*Acclaim for*

# SAM SHEPARD

"Sam Shepard is phenomenal . . . the best practicing American playwright."
—*The New Republic*

"The greatest American playwright of his generation . . . the most inventive in language and revolutionary in craft."
—*New York* magazine

"His plays are a form of exorcism: magical, sometimes surreal rituals that grapple with demonic forces in the American landscape."
—*Newsweek*

"His plays are stunning in their originality, defiant and inscrutable."
—*Esquire*

"With the exception of David Mamet, no American playwright of his generation matches Mr. Shepard in the creation of characters that are immediately so accessible and so mysterious."
—*The New York Times*

"One of the most original, prolific and gifted dramatists at work today."
—*The New Yorker*

SAM   SHEPARD

# *Simpatico*

Sam Shepard has written forty-five plays, eleven of which
have won Obie Awards, and has appeared as an actor in
sixteen films. In 1979 he was awarded the Pulitzer Prize for
Drama for *Buried Child*, and in 1984 he gained an Oscar
nomination for his performance in *The Right Stuff*. His
screenplay for *Paris, Texas* won the Golden Palm Award at
the 1984 Cannes Film Festival, and he wrote and directed
the film *Far North* in 1988. Other plays by Sam Shepard
include *Simpatico*, *Curse of the Starving Class*, *True West*, *Fool
for Love*, and *A Lie of the Mind*. In 1986 he was elected to
the American Academy of Arts and Letters, and in 1992 he
received the Gold Medal for Drama from the Academy. In
1994 he was inducted into the Theatre Hall of Fame.

ALSO BY SAM SHEPARD

*Cruising Paradise*

*States of Shock, Far North, Silent Tongue*

*The Unseen Hand*

*A Lie of the Mind*

*Fool for Love*

*Paris, Texas*

*Seven Plays*

*Motel Chronicles*

*Hawk Moon*

# Simpatico

# SAM SHEPARD

# *Simpatico*

## A PLAY IN THREE ACTS

VINTAGE BOOKS
A DIVISION OF RANDOM HOUSE, INC.
NEW YORK

FIRST VINTAGE BOOKS EDITION, MAY 1996

*Copyright © 1995 by Sam Shepard*

All rights reserved under International and Pan-American
Copyright Conventions. Published in the United States by
Vintage Books, a division of Random House, Inc., New York,
and simultaneously in Canada by Random House of
Canada Limited, Toronto. Originally published in
Great Britain in paperback in the
Royal Court Writers series by
Methuen Drama, an imprint
of Reed Books Ltd.,
London, in 1995.

Library of Congress Cataloging-in-Publication Data
Shepard, Sam, 1943–
Simpatico: a play in three acts / Sam Shepard. — 1st Vintage Books ed.
p. cm.
ISBN 0-679-76317-1
I. Title.
PS3569.H394S56 1996
812'.54—dc20 95-43451
CIP

Random House Web address: http://www.randomhouse.com/

Printed in the United States of America
10  9  8  7  6  5

*Simpatico*

*Simpatico* was first presented at the Joseph Papp Public Theater in New York, on November 14, 1994. The cast was as follows:

|  |  |
|---:|:---|
| CARTER: | Ed Harris |
| VINNIE: | Fred Ward |
| CECILIA: | Marcia Gay Harden |
| SIMMS: | James Gammon |
| KELLY: | Welker White |
| ROSIE: | Beverly D'Angelo |

|  |  |
|---:|:---|
| *Directed by* | Sam Shepard |
| *Designed by* | Loy Arcenas |
| *Lighting by* | Anne Militello |
| *Music by* | Patrick O'Hearn |
| *Sound by* | Tom Morse |

ACT 1 Cucamonga, California

ACT 2 San Dimas, California; Midway, Kentucky; Cucamonga, California

ACT 3 Lexington, Kentucky; Midway, Kentucky; Cucamonga, California

# Act One

Scene: Lights come up on—a cheap, ground-floor apartment on the outskirts of Cucamonga. A sign with this single place-name, "CUCAMONGA", hangs above the set. The apartment is very sparse. A sink piled with dirty dishes against the stage-right wall. A bed with one blanket against the left wall. A pile of dirty clothes at the foot of the bed, on the floor. Rough stucco walls in pale green, absolutely bare with no attempt to decorate. A window in each wall trimmed in pale Mexican orange with sun-bleached plastic curtains. The windows look out into black space. No trees. No buildings. No landscape of any kind. Just black.

Note: This set occupies most of the stage in Act One. In Acts Two and Three it takes up only part of the stage, on the stage-right side.

Actors have entered in the dark. Lights come up on VINNIE, sitting on the edge of the bed, elbows on knees, staring at the floor. He's dressed in a dark blue long-sleeved shirt, dark slacks with no belt. Everything very rumpled as though he's been sleeping in his clothes for weeks. Bare feet. CARTER peruses the room, crossing from one window to the next, looking out, then moving to the sink. He's dressed in a very expensive beige suit, dark tie, brown overcoat slung over one arm and a briefcase containing his cellular phone. His shoes are alligator loafers with little tassels. Both men are well into their forties.

CARTER: Well, this isn't bad, Vinnie. Cozy. Close to the

mall. Little sparse maybe. Picture I had was that you were much worse off.

VINNIE: What's sparse about it?

CARTER: Well—it could use a lady's touch. You know—a few throw-rugs or something. What do they call those? You know—throw-rugs.

VINNIE: All's I need is a bed.

CARTER: Sixties style, huh?

VINNIE: I didn't have a bed in the sixties.

*Pause.*

CARTER: Right. Well, you got someone looking after you? Someone to do the laundry? Dishes? I can get that arranged for you if you want. Local talent.

VINNIE: I'm fine.

CARTER: Okay. (*Moves to pile of laundry.*) But you shouldn't ought to let the laundry pile up on you, Vinnie. You let that happen, it starts to go sour. Gives you a bad impression of yourself.

VINNIE: I don't need the laundry for that.

*Pause.*

CARTER: You taking care of yourself otherwise? Not too much booze?

VINNIE: Not *too* much.

CARTER: Get out for a uh—stroll now and then? Fresh air. Blood pumping?

VINNIE: I walk everywhere.

CARTER: Good! That's good. Gotta keep your health up. Funny how the mind follows the body. Ever noticed that? You get sick, first thing you know the mind starts going straight to hell.

VINNIE: I walked clear to Glendora yesterday.

CARTER: Glendora?

VINNIE: Yeah. Clear to Glendora and back.

CARTER: That's quite a hike—Glendora. Out near where Shoemaker had his big wreck isn't it?

VINNIE: You know very well where Glendora is.

CARTER: What happened to that car I bought you?

VINNIE: Sold it.

CARTER: Why'd you do that?

VINNIE: Jap car.

CARTER: Well, you shoulda told me what you wanted, Vinnie. I could've got you an American car easy enough. Little Jeep Cherokee or something. All you gotta do is ask.

VINNIE: Cherokees flip. They're unstable.

CARTER: Well, a Mustang then or—

VINNIE: I don't need a car. I walk. Ever since I lost my Buick I walk.

*Pause.*

CARTER: Okay. Just seems like you might need some wheels to get around out here, that's all. We always used to.

VINNIE: I don't.

CARTER: All right. Good. Fair enough. I'm just trying to look out for you, Vinnie. (*Pause.*) Everything okay otherwise? Need some more cash? New shirts? You got that TV I sent you, didn't you?

VINNIE: Sold that too.

*Small pause.*

CARTER: They don't make American TVs anymore, Vinnie. They don't exist. They haven't made a purebred American TV for over forty years now.

VINNIE: I know that. "RCA".

CARTER: Whatever.

VINNIE: "His Master's Voice".

CARTER: Yeah—

VINNIE: Who was his Master anyway?

CARTER: Look—You wanted to talk to me, right? You called me. You've got some kind of a major crisis going on. Something that couldn't wait.

VINNIE: I do. Crisis is my middle name.

CARTER: I flew all the way out here just to talk to you, Vinnie. Do you wanna talk or do you wanna be cryptic and weird?

VINNIE: I appreciate that.

CARTER: What.

VINNIE: That you came all the way out here. Just to talk. I appreciate that.

CARTER: No problem. Our friendship always comes first. You know that. Always has.

VINNIE: If you say so.

CARTER: I do.

VINNIE: I haven't asked you for much special treatment over the years, have I Carter?

CARTER: No you haven't. You've been very understanding about this whole business.

VINNIE: Never called you collect in the middle of the night.

CARTER: Never.

VINNIE: Never interfered with your private life.

CARTER: No.

VINNIE: I've been extremely discreet.

CARTER: You have, Vinnie.

VINNIE: I've been a good boy.

CARTER: Yes.

VINNIE: Because I could really hurt you if I wanted to—

CARTER: All right, look Vinnie—let's—

VINNIE: I could demolish you if I really had a mind to. You haven't forgotten that have you?

CARTER: No! (*Pause.*) I haven't forgotten that.

VINNIE: Good. (*Pause.*) I still own all the negatives, you know. I still have them in my possession. All the early correspondence.

CARTER: Could we just get down to this problem you're having. This big problem that couldn't wait.

VINNIE: I'm not holding you up or anything am I?

CARTER: I've got to catch a return flight in about two hours.

VINNIE: Returning to the family?

CARTER: That's right.

VINNIE: Little wife? Little lady?

CARTER: Hey, don't think you can trot right across my head, pal! Just because you did me a couple a' crumby favors a long time ago.

VINNIE: Favors?

CARTER: A *long*, long time ago! (*Pause.*) There's certain limits—certain parameters. I'm not gonna be blackmailed, Vinnie.

VINNIE: Farthest thing from my mind.

CARTER: Good. Now, what's the problem?

*Pause.*

VINNIE: Uh—I got arrested about a week ago.

CARTER: Oh great! That's just wonderful! Arrested! Now you've gotten yourself arrested!

VINNIE: Don't worry. Nothing showed up on the records. No trace of you anywhere. No trace of Simms. You've been very thorough about all that.

CARTER: What'd you get arrested for?

VINNIE: It was—kind of multiple charges.

CARTER: Terrific.

VINNIE: "Trespassing". "Invasion of Privacy". And uh—"Harassment".

CARTER: Harassment?

VINNIE: Yeah. Harassment.

CARTER: You didn't assault anyone, did you?

VINNIE: No. I don't do that. That's not my specialty. You know that.

CARTER: Who'd you harass then?

VINNIE: No one.

CARTER: All right—Who *charged* you with harassment?

VINNIE: A woman.

CARTER: Here we go—

VINNIE: But it won't stick. Told me to stay away from her house. Hysterical reaction on her part, is all it was. Petty-anti stuff.

CARTER: Hysterical reaction to what?

VINNIE: She felt I'd deceived her, I guess.

CARTER: Deception is not harassment.

VINNIE: Exactly *my* point.

CARTER: What else did you do to her?

VINNIE: Nothing. I didn't touch her. We never even kissed. Never hugged even.

CARTER: So, it's just a uh—"psychological" thing with her, I suppose. Same old, same old.

VINNIE: Must be. I can't figure it out.

CARTER: What's the "Trespassing" deal? The "Invasion of Privacy"?

VINNIE: Uh—See, I had her believing that I was a detective.

CARTER: Oh, Vinnie—

VINNIE: A real detective. She was absolutely convinced.

CARTER: That's the *deception* part. I'm talking about the—

VINNIE: She went right along with it. I showed her my badge, handcuffs, the gun, false ID. She got very excited about the whole thing.

CARTER: You're not carrying a weapon again are you?

VINNIE: Only on dates.

CARTER: You can't take chances like that, Vinnie. Walking around here with a weapon. Did they find it on you?

VINNIE: No. I ditched it. I'm very good at that. You know that. Went back two days later and picked it up, right where I'd left it.

CARTER: You can't take those kind of risks! I've told you that.

VINNIE: Not now anyway.

CARTER: That's right.

VINNIE: There was a time and place for risks and that time has passed.

CARTER: That's what *I've* said!

VINNIE: I was just repeating it. Just to reassure you that I've absorbed your instructions.

*Pause.*

CARTER (*with patience*): *Where* did you trespass and *whose* privacy did you invade?

VINNIE: I met this woman—

CARTER: We're going backwards, Vinnie.

VINNIE: You'll have to bear with me. You've got no choice.

*Pause.*

CARTER: All right.

VINNIE: I met this woman—like I said. Watched her walk into the bar.

CARTER: I thought you weren't drinking these days.

VINNIE (*sudden violent explosion*): NOT TOO MUCH, I SAID!! NOT TOO MUCH!! (*Pause into sudden calm.*) You're not listening.

CARTER: I am.

VINNIE (*calm*): You're interrupting. You've got to pay close attention to this. Try to grasp all the details.

CARTER: I am. Take it easy. I'm just asking.

VINNIE: I watched her. She had a movement to her. A kind of life. Like a dog caught in the headlights.

CARTER: A dog caught in the headlights?

VINNIE: Similar to that.

CARTER: You were *attracted* to her. In so many words.

VINNIE: I was. I admit that. I'm not ashamed to admit that. I had a thought. A thought came into my head as soon as I saw her and I'd never had this kind of thought before. I said to myself: "If I could have this woman—I would never ever ask for anything else again in my whole life." I said to myself: "Please, dear God in Heaven, deliver this woman to me and I will never pester you again for anything whatsoever. For all Eternity I will leave you alone." (*Pause.*) And a miraculous thing occurred.

CARTER: What was that?

VINNIE: She came straight over to me. As though I'd called her. As though I'd conjured her up. Sat down right next to me and smiled. Just like she was answering my little prayer.

CARTER: Congratulations. So, then what? You started the scam on her? The "detective" scam? I can't believe you're still doing this, Vinnie.

VINNIE: She asked me what I do for a living. Right off the bat. Very sincere eyes. Well, you know, that's the one question that always throws me.

CARTER: What's that?

VINNIE: The question of "occupation". What I *do* for a living.

CARTER: I've offered you all kinds of jobs over the years, Vinnie. All kinds of opportunities.

VINNIE: I worked for you once. Once was enough.

CARTER: That was a partnership! We were absolutely equal.

VINNIE: Could I continue my story? Please.

*Pause.*

CARTER: I thought you'd given all this up, Vinnie. You told me you'd stopped doing this.

VINNIE: What.

CARTER: All this business with women. Pretending.

VINNIE: It's not a business!

CARTER: How many times have you gotten yourself into a jam like this over a woman?

VINNIE: Never. Not like this.

CARTER: Oh, this one's different. I see.

VINNIE: Are you listening to me or scolding me!

CARTER: I'm *telling* you! This is *exactly* what I've been warning you about all these years. One little slip-up like this and the whole thing can come unraveled.

VINNIE: There's no way they can connect you to me.

CARTER: When you apply for a State Racing License what is the main prerequisite? Fingerprints! Right? Fingerprints, Vinnie! You've got no concept of how things are hooked up these days. How international files are kept. Information stored. Microchips. Fibre optics. Floppy discs. It's an art form now, Vinnie! An industry!

VINNIE (*sudden explosion again*): I AM TALKING ABOUT A WOMAN!!

*Pause.*

CARTER: All right. Calm down. Jesus. We're just trying to have a conversation.

VINNIE: I AM NOT TALKING ABOUT MICROCHIPS AND INDUSTRIES!! I AM TALKING ABOUT A WOMAN!!

CARTER: If you're going to scream, I'm going to leave.

VINNIE (*calmer*): You're not listening to me, I don't think.

CARTER: I am.

VINNIE: I don't think so.

CARTER: I am. It's just—

VINNIE: So, tell me what I'm saying then. Tell me back.

*Pause.*

CARTER: You wanna take a walk? Go out and have a drink somewhere? Get some air?

VINNIE: Tell me what I'm saying. I'd like to hear it. Back.

CARTER: Let's have a drink.

VINNIE: *You* don't drink. Remember?

CARTER (*pause*): I've taken it up again.

VINNIE: Oh? Things not so hot back home?

CARTER: What?

VINNIE: I said: (*As though speaking to the deaf.*) "THINGS—NOT—SO—HOT—BACK—AT—HOME?"

CARTER: Everything's fine. I just have an occasional highball to take the edge off. Just to relax. That's all.

VINNIE: Ah, the Occasional Highball!

CARTER: Whatever, Whiskey sour. Now and then.

VINNIE: No harm in that.

CARTER: None whatsoever.

VINNIE: Kids back in school are they?

CARTER: They start this week.

VINNIE: It's that time of year. PUMPKIN TIME!

CARTER: Yeah.

VINNIE: Rosie's happy?

CARTER: I'd just as soon not talk about Rosie, if you don't mind.

VINNIE: She still got those amazing tits that kinda sit up like little puppy dogs and bark at you?

CARTER *charges* VINNIE, *grabs him by the throat and throws him backwards onto the bed, then smashes him with the pillow.* VINNIE *smiles and lays there passively while* CARTER *stands over him. Long pause.* CARTER *backs off.*

VINNIE (*sitting up on bed, smiling*): So—You're back on the bottle my good man. I happen to have some of that Northern Irish stuff. "Black Bush". The best.

VINNIE *reaches under bed, pulls out bottle of bourbon and a short glass. Pours himself a drink as they continue.*

CARTER: No thanks.

VINNIE: Too rough? Black Bush can be pretty rough if all you've been used to is the "Occasional Highball".

CARTER: Are you going to finish telling me about this woman?

VINNIE: You're not listening, Carter. Your mind is elsewhere.

CARTER: Just don't talk about my wife, okay?

VINNIE: *Your* wife?

CARTER: That's right!

VINNIE: I was just curious is all. We go off in different directions. Lota time goes by. Lota water under the bridge. You can't help but wonder.

CARTER: Wonder to yourself.

VINNIE: Green swimming pool. White Mercedez. Blue car phone. Must have a phone in every car, right Carter? Every bathroom. Keep track a' things while you're taking a dump. Cellular business. How is business these days?

CARTER: Market's down. The Arabs have dropped out of the game.

VINNIE: But the Japs—the Japs are coming on strong.

CARTER: Not strong enough.

VINNIE: The rich are clamping down!

*Pause.*

CARTER: Look, Vinnie. I gave you all kinds of options. I mean—

VINNIE: Options!

CARTER: I did. At one point in time you could have—

VINNIE: The option to disappear, for instance. The option to perpetually change my name and address. The option to live like a ghost.

CARTER: Look—You're here, you're alive. You're not in jail. So far anyway.

VINNIE: Three pluses in your book!

CARTER: Better than dead, Vinnie. Better than being locked away.

VINNIE (*sudden quiet sincerity*): I *am* dead. I *am* locked away.

*Pause.*

CARTER: Maybe you'd be better off in Europe. What do you think? Did you ever think of Europe? We could set you up over there. Some little obscure village tucked away in Austria, maybe.

VINNIE: What am I gonna do tucked away in Austria? Ski? Yodel, maybe?

CARTER: I don't know—

VINNIE: I'll tell you what the option is. Here's an option. You turn yourself in, Carter.

CARTER: Hey!

VINNIE: You walk right into the FBI and confess the whole fandango. Lay all your cards on the table. Worst they'll give you is a slap on the wrist and a little fine. Man of your position.

CARTER: What the hell good is that gonna do? What're you saying?

VINNIE: Let me off the hook.

CARTER: Let yourself off the hook. I'm not your jailer.

VINNIE: Let me off the hook, Carter!

*Pause.*

CARTER: I'm—perfectly willing to help you out in any way I can. You know that, Vinnie. I always have been. That's why I'm here, now. But—

VINNIE: You're here, *now*, because you're scared and guilty. That's why you're here, *now*.

CARTER (*laughing*): Scared and guilty?

VINNIE: One or the other. Or both.

CARTER: Scared and guilty!

VINNIE: Neither one is the right motive.

CARTER: Oh, well, I apologize for that!

VINNIE: Neither one has to do with kinship or brotherhood or any sense of another man's suffering at the hands of a woman.

CARTER: Oh, so now we're suffering! We're suffering now!

VINNIE: One of us might be suffering!

CARTER: But the other one has no conception of it! Is that the idea!

VINNIE: That's the idea but the idea is a long way from the truth!

CARTER: Aah! The Truth! The Truth! And only one of us is able to have a handle on that I suppose!

VINNIE: One of us is a helluva lot closer to it than the other one!

CARTER: And the other one is just blindly staggering! Just bashing into walls, leaving carnage in his wake!

VINNIE (*pause*): One of us has forgotten.

*Pause.*

CARTER: What do you want me to do, Vinnie? You want me to talk to this girl? Straighten something out? What exactly do you want me to do?

VINNIE: It was just a uh—wild impulse.

CARTER: What was?

VINNIE: Calling you up. Thinking there was some remote possibility that you might—have an answer.

CARTER: I'm not any better at figuring out women than you are, Vinnie.

VINNIE: No, I suppose not. After all, look who you ended up marrying.

CARTER: Look—

VINNIE: Does she ever pull that on you, Carter? The cold-shoulder routine? She could make a rock cry.

CARTER: I am *not* going to get into a conversation about Rosie!

VINNIE: She used to pull that on me. All the time. 'Course she never went so far as to have me arrested. You've never been arrested have you, Carter?

CARTER: No. I never have.

VINNIE: There's plenty of good reasons why you *should* be arrested: extortion, kickbacks, third-party transfers, money laundering—

CARTER: Hey, goddammit!

VINNIE: But, for some reason, you never were. Call it luck. Let's call it luck, shall we?

CARTER: Luck had nothing to do with it. We were both well aware of the risks going into it.

VINNIE: Even Rosie—

CARTER: Leave her out of this!

VINNIE: Even Rosie was well aware.

CARTER: I'm walking out the door, Vinnie! I'm walking!

VINNIE: No you're not. You're in no position to threaten me. I'm the one holding all the cards, Carter. I'm the one and only one who can call you any time of the day or night and have you book your ass out here to the edge of nowhere. Who else can do that? Does anybody else have that kind of power in your "organization"?

CARTER: You're not going to expose me. You want me to believe that? You're tied into Simms' dismissal every bit as much as me.

VINNIE: You made sure of that, didn't you?

CARTER: It was *you* who took the photographs, for Christ's sake!

VINNIE: And *you* who set him up!

CARTER: He didn't need setting up! There was more corruption in his commission than anything we could've ever cooked up ourselves. All we did was document the truth. I've got no regrets about that, believe you me. No regrets whatsoever. Simms hung himself.

VINNIE: Document the truth?

CARTER: That's right!

VINNIE: *I* took the photographs, Carter. I saw what I was shooting!

CARTER: Nobody twisted your arm either.

VINNIE: Would you like to see them again to refresh your memory?

CARTER: No! I would *not* like to see them again!

VINNIE: I didn't think so.

CARTER: Nobody coerced you into taking those pictures, Vinnie. You were a free agent.

*Pause.*

VINNIE: What was in it for me? I forgot that part. There must have been something. Something rewarding.

CARTER: Is that what this is all about? Your reward? If you want me to increase your monthly deposit that can be arranged, Vinnie. That's easy. Just come out and say it and stop tap-dancing around.

*Pause.*

VINNIE: Are you a member of a country club out there?

CARTER: What?

VINNIE: Are you a member of a country club out there?

CARTER: Out where?

VINNIE: Out there in the "Blue Grass Country" where you've forged a brand new life for yourself and your cute little wife.

CARTER: A country club?

VINNIE: Yeah. Are you a member of one? It's a relatively straightforward question.

CARTER: What's that got to do with anything!

VINNIE: I bet you are, aren't you?

CARTER: Yeah! Yeah, I'm a member of a country club! So fuckin' what!

VINNIE: Well, that must be something new and different for you, huh? Being a member. Must've been difficult at first. Fitting in. Pretending you had something in common. Kissing ass with the gentry.

CARTER: I don't have time to screw around here, Vinnie.

VINNIE: But now it's become second nature, right? You've acquired an affinity. You stride right through the pro-shop on your way to the bar, laughing and slapping all your divorced buddies on the butt. Cracking inane jokes about pussy you've never had. Collecting football pools and swapping putters. Like your seedy past is long forgot. Might never have really even taken place. Might have actually belonged to another man. A man so remote and dead to you that you've lost all connection. A man completely sacrificed in honor of your bogus membership in the High Life.

CARTER: Nobody forced you into a hole, Vinnie! Nobody!

VINNIE: Nobody did! It must've been DESTINY!

CARTER: Nobody demanded you screw yourself up with women and booze and lying and pretending—

VINNIE: LYING!

*Long pause.*

CARTER: I've gotta go.

VINNIE: You should. The kids'll be late for school!

*Pause.*

CARTER: I can't keep this up, Vinnie. It's a dead end. Every time it's a dead end.

VINNIE: Kinda like marriage, isn't it?

CARTER: Worse.

VINNIE: Well—

CARTER: I get this—sickening feeling that it'll never end.

VINNIE: It's a *lot* like marriage.

CARTER: We just go around and around and around—

VINNIE: It *has* been going on for a spell, hasn't it? Old pal, old buddy, old friend of mine.

*Pause.*

CARTER: What do you want from me, Vinnie? I've tried to take care of you. I really have.

VINNIE: Yeah. I guess you have.

CARTER: I mean, I don't know what else to do except give you more money. Buy you stuff. Move you to a different place. What else do you want me to do?

VINNIE: Come clean, Carter. It's real simple.

*Pause.*

CARTER: Look—I've got a proposition to make you.

VINNIE: A proposition!

CARTER: I'm prepared to make you an offer. You name me a price. Just name me a price—a *realistic* price and I'll pay you *cash* for all the stuff you've got on me. All the negatives, letters, tapes, whatever you've got. We'll clean this whole mess up, once and for all, and be done with it.

VINNIE: But then we'd never see each other again, Carter.

CARTER: I'm serious, Vinnie! I want to end this thing!

*Pause.*

VINNIE: You're the only friend I've got, Carter. I mean—this girl—This girl isn't gonna work out. I can tell she's not gonna work out.

CARTER: You don't know that. All you've got to do is go talk to her. I mean if you've got that much feeling for her—

VINNIE: SHE WON'T TALK TO ME! She had me arrested! It wasn't any fun being arrested. I mean I'm not a criminal!

CARTER: No, you're not.

VINNIE: I'm not a criminal in the common sense!

CARTER: Of course not.

VINNIE: Not like you. I mean, I'm basically innocent. I'm an intrinsically innocent person, Carter!

CARTER: Try to calm down.

VINNIE: All I was doing was trying to impress her. That's all. I might have gone a little overboard with the gun and the handcuffs but I wasn't trying to hurt her. She had no reason to arrest me, Carter!

CARTER: No, she didn't.

*Pause.*

VINNIE: It's a terrible thing—trying to replace someone— You know? Trying to find someone to take the place—I mean—see, after Rosie ran off I just kinda—(*Takes a drink.*)

CARTER: She didn't "run off"

VINNIE: She didn't?

CARTER: No.

VINNIE: What would you call it?

CARTER: She—eloped.

VINNIE: Oh! "Eloped"! *That's* what you call it. That's right. "Eloped"!

CARTER: Well, she didn't "run off". That makes her sound sneaky and deceitful. That just wasn't the case.

VINNIE: "Eloped". (*Offers* CARTER *a drink.*) Drink?

CARTER *refuses drink.*

VINNIE: Takes two to elope, I guess. That must be the difference. If it's only just one person eloping then you might call it "running off".

CARTER: You might.

*Pause.*

VINNIE: Where—did you elope *to* when you both "eloped"?

CARTER: You're bound and determined to get it around to Rosie, aren't you. You can't help yourself.

VINNIE: Well, it's the main thing we share in common these days, isn't it, Carter?

CARTER: I didn't come here to talk about Rosie.

VINNIE: I'm just curious. Again. In a state of wonder. I used to wonder about it all the time. It was my constant obsession. I'd wake up with it heavy on my mind. The two of you alone in the Buick. Highway 40 East. Driving through the night with her neck on your shoulder. Tucumcari. Amarillo. The smell of cattle in the feedlots. Oil on the wind. The lights of Memphis twinkling across the placid Mississippi.

CARTER: It wasn't that poetic. Believe me.

VINNIE: No?

CARTER: No! It wasn't. I mean—it may have started off that way—

VINNIE: That was *my* Buick too. You realize that, don't you? *My* Buick and *my* wife.

CARTER: It was *her* choice, Vinnie. I never—(*Stops himself.*)

*Pause.*

VINNIE: What? You never what?

CARTER: One thing—just led to another. It was *her* idea to run away together, not mine.

VINNIE: "Elope".

*Pause.*

CARTER: Yes.

VINNIE: You were a victim of circumstance?

CARTER: Well—

VINNIE: And it all just happened to coincide with our little scam on Simms, I guess. That was convenient.

CARTER: It had nothing to do with that!

VINNIE: My forced exile!

CARTER: She had made it up in her mind a long time before that!

*Pause.*

VINNIE: Oh. Is that right?

CARTER: Yes. That's right.

VINNIE: How long before?

CARTER: Look—

VINNIE: How long!

CARTER: I don't know how long! Months maybe.

VINNIE: Months? For months you were both sneaking around! Boffing each other in the back seat of my Buick while I was out steadfastly hustling your dirty work! Preparing the ground for your Big Success!

CARTER: No! It was nothing like that. It came out of nowhere.

VINNIE: One day she just woke up and realized she was with the wrong man? That must've been it, huh? A sudden revelation. That happens sometimes. That happened to me once. A sudden revelation.

*Pause.* CARTER *goes to* VINNIE, *takes bottle from him and takes a belt straight from the bottle.*

VINNIE: Would you like a glass?

CARTER: No.

CARTER *hands bottle back to* VINNIE.

VINNIE: I don't blame her a bit, actually, Carter. Tell you the truth. You were on a roll. Unstoppable. I thought you might even end up running for Congress. Smooching babies and waving from cabooses. You had that aura about you. A kind of uh—yuppie Protestant aura, that's become so popular these days.

CARTER: It caught me by surprise, Vinnie. I was as shocked by it as you were.

VINNIE: I doubt it.

CARTER: I didn't even realize I had any feelings for her until—she just—opened up to me, I guess. She seemed so—

VINNIE: Desperate?

CARTER: Yeah. She did. Desperate and vulnerable at the same time.

VINNIE: A deadly combination.

CARTER: It just caught me completely off-guard.

VINNIE: Yeah. She pulled that on me too. In the beginning. All wide-eyed and bushy-tailed.

CARTER: But it wasn't like a game with her or anything—not like *you* pretending to be a detective. She—

VINNIE: I never pretended with Rosie.

CARTER: No, but you know what I mean.

VINNIE: I know what you mean but I never pretended with her. I never *had* to pretend with Rosie.

CARTER: All right—

VINNIE: You're not trying to imply that me and her had some superficial thing going, are you?

CARTER: No, I'm just saying—

VINNIE: That suddenly *you* came along and she saw the light?

CARTER: No! She seemed to have this idea in her head. And I don't know where it came from.

VINNIE: What idea?

CARTER: That I was her—ticket—out. I guess.

VINNIE: Well, you were, weren't you? She got what she wanted.

CARTER: No. No, she didn't.

VINNIE: Oh. Well, what happened, Carter? Come on. You can tell me. We're old buddies. Confidants. We've been through the wars together.

CARTER: I don't know what happened.

VINNIE: Things went sour?

CARTER: Yeah. Very suddenly.

VINNIE: Things went a little limp in the sack, did they?

CARTER: No. She—(*Stops himself.*)

VINNIE: What?

CARTER: I've gotta get going, Vinnie. I really do.

VINNIE: Hang on, hang on. She found someone else. Is that it?

CARTER: No!

VINNIE: Here, take another pull.

> VINNIE *offers* CARTER *the bottle.* CARTER *takes it and drinks, hands it back.*

CARTER: I didn't want to get into this!

VINNIE: Well, I didn't realize there was any big trauma. I thought you and Rosie were—

CARTER: We're not!

VINNIE: You wanna—sit down and talk about it?

CARTER: No! I do *not* want to sit down and talk about it! I've got no business here! I've gotta get back. I don't have time to fuck around here with your personal problems, Vinnie!

VINNIE: *My* personal problems?

CARTER: That's right. That's why I'm out here, in case you forgot.

VINNIE: Well, maybe I could help you out, Carter.

CARTER: You?

VINNIE: Yeah. Maybe I could help you out with Rosie. I don't know.

CARTER: *You* could help *me* out with Rosie? What is wrong with you, Vinnie?

VINNIE: I don't know. Seems like it'd be a fair exchange. I help you out with Rosie, you could help me out with Cecilia.

CARTER: Cecilia?

VINNIE: This girl.

CARTER: The one who had you popped?

VINNIE: Yeah. That one.

CARTER: I don't know how your mind operates, Vinnie. You don't give two shits about this girl, do you? You're just looking for a way to sabotage me.

VINNIE: Sabotage you?

CARTER: Yeah! Plotting behind my back. What else have you got to do, laying around here with your bottle and your bullshit detective paraphernalia? Dream up ways stab me in the back!

VINNIE: I was just making an offer, Carter. That's all I was doing. A friendly gesture. I know how—painful it can be, see—When things—fall apart.

*Pause.*

CARTER: I am leaving, Vinnie! I am walking out this door and you can take all the junk you've supposedly got on me and turn it in.

VINNIE: You don't want me to do that.

CARTER: Gather it all up and trundle it down to the local PD! Tell them your amazing tale! Tell them how come you've waited fifteen years before you revealed all the slimey facts! Tell them how much you want to go to prison right along with me! I'm sure they'll be more than willing to re-open the case. There's such a scarcity of dramatic crime these days!

VINNIE: I'll make you a deal.

CARTER: Oh, now you're gonna make *me* a deal? Stick it where it fits, Vinnie!

VINNIE: Just listen to me.

CARTER: I made you an offer but all you wanna do is jerk me around! Play this little psycho-game of how you're really the big dog pushing all the buttons. All you are is a scumbag fugitive from the law, Vinnie! A fleeing felon! That's all you are. A low-life punk who gets busted for harassing women. Good luck, pal.

VINNIE: No wait! Just hang on a second.

CARTER: You can't hurt me, Vinnie. You've hurt yourself too much.

VINNIE: Just do me one favor, okay? One last favor. I haven't asked you for many favors over the years, have I?

CARTER: Are you begging now?

VINNIE: Yeah. Yeah, I guess I am.

CARTER: You're begging. That's better.

VINNIE: Yeah.

CARTER: That's more in line with how it should be.

VINNIE: Yeah. Yeah, I guess you're right.

CARTER: What kinda favor do you want, Vinnie?

VINNIE: I got—used to talking to this girl. I liked talking to her. She's—nice, ya know. She's not Rosie but she's—nice.

CARTER: A *nice* girl.

VINNIE: Yeah.

CARTER: And you want me to tell her what a nice guy *you* are, right? What a sweetheart you are, deep down.

VINNIE: You don't have to lie. Just—

CARTER: Make up a story.

VINNIE: Tell her—how I used to be.

CARTER: When was that?

VINNIE: Back—you know—When we were runnin' claimers. In the old days, you know.

CARTER: Oh yeah. You were pretty nice back then.

VINNIE: We had some laughs.

CARTER: We did.

VINNIE: Tell her how we used to swap those two geldings around—you know. How the money was flying.

CARTER: Back before Simms got wind of it, you mean?

VINNIE: Don't mention anything about him. There's no reason to.

CARTER: He's changed his name, you know.

VINNIE: Simms?

CARTER: Yeah. I set him up with a bloodstock agency back there. Selling seasons and shares. Dabbling in pedigrees. He's doing all right for himself.

VINNIE: Changed his name?

CARTER: Calls himself "Ames" or something. Ryan Ames, I think it is.

VINNIE: Seasons and shares? Simms?

CARTER: Yeah. What's so surprising about that? He was always very industrious.

VINNIE: So that means there's two of us collecting hush money off you?

CARTER: It's not hush money! I just thought it was the least I could do for him, after he—stepped aside.

VINNIE: Well, he must've been very grateful. How much do you give *him* a month?

CARTER: I don't *give* him anything! He's got a job. He's independent.

VINNIE: Does he get more than I do?

CARTER: He's got nothing but a job, Vinnie! That's all. An opportunity to put himself back on track. The difference is that *he* took advantage of it.

VINNIE: The difference?

CARTER: Between you and him.

VINNIE: Oh, yeah.

CARTER: Now what's this big favor?

VINNIE: What?

CARTER: With the girl—Cynthia or whatever her name is.

VINNIE: Cecilia.

CARTER: Cecilia, yeah.

VINNIE: I can't believe Simms is back in the mainstream, selling seasons and shares. Doesn't anybody recognize him?

CARTER: He changed his name.

VINNIE: "Ames"? "Ryan Ames"? What is he, impersonating an Irishman or something? Right in the middle of Lexington?

CARTER: Midway.

VINNIE: Ah. Midway. So you've got him tucked away too.

CARTER: Some people have the capacity to take their knocks and keep on going, Vinnie.

VINNIE: I guess—Midway. That's quaint.

CARTER: Some people even get stronger from it.

VINNIE: I tried, Carter. It wasn't from a lack of trying. I've changed my name a dozen times and nothing came of it. I've moved all over the place. I was in Texas for a while, remember? Arizona. Nothing came from any of it. I just got—further and further—removed.

CARTER: Well, let me try to talk to this girl for you.

VINNIE: I don't know. I don't know if she's the answer. I mean—

CARTER: Let me just talk to her. She might come around.

VINNIE: I was thinking, you know—What I was going to tell you was that if you could get her to change her mind about me—Maybe get her to come over here and talk to me about the whole business—What I was thinking was—

CARTER: What?

VINNIE: That I'd hand over all—the stuff. Let you have it.

CARTER: All the negatives?

VINNIE: Everything.

CARTER: You've still got it all?

VINNIE: Yeah. It's all in a shoe-box. It's all stacked very neatly in there. Not a speck of dust on anything. I check it all on a regular basis.

CARTER: Good.

VINNIE: I check it every night before I go to bed. Some of— the letters—kinda take me back.

CARTER: You still have them? All the letters?

VINNIE: Every one.

CARTER: All the pictures?

VINNIE: Yeah. All but a couple.

CARTER: There's a couple missing?

VINNIE: Two. Yeah. But I know where they are.

CARTER: You *gave* them to someone?

VINNIE: It's all right.

CARTER: Who'd you give them to, Vinnie?

VINNIE: It's all right.

CARTER: WHO'D YOU GIVE THEM TO!

VINNIE: Cecilia. She has them. She's got them in a safe place.

CARTER: Why'd you give them to Cecilia, Vinnie!

VINNIE: Just—I loaned them to her as proof.

CARTER: Proof of what?

VINNIE: That I actually *am* a detective.

*Pause.*

CARTER: Give me her address.

VINNIE: You're gonna talk to her?

CARTER: Just—give me the address, Vinnie!

VINNIE: You're gonna talk to her about me or are you gonna ask her for the pictures back?

CARTER: I'm going to talk to her about you. I'm going to, very calmly, explain to her the roots of your particular insanity.

VINNIE: No, don't tell her that. She already thinks I'm crazy.

CARTER: She's right.

VINNIE: That's not gonna help! I don't want her coming over here out of pity!

CARTER: What difference does it make why she comes? Once she's here you can line things out with her. Vindicate yourself.

VINNIE: *I AM NOT GUILTY!!*

*Pause.*

CARTER: No. No, you're not, Vinnie. And I'll make sure she understands that. I'll make sure she sees that your downfall was the result of bad company. Nothing else. Just plain old bad company.

*Pause.* CARTER *moves downstage, then suddenly remembers something and turns to* VINNIE.

CARTER: What year was that Buick, anyway? You remember?

VINNIE: '58.

CARTER: '58. Well, maybe I'll try to find you another one, Vinnie.

*Blackout.*

# Act Two

## SCENE ONE

*Stage is divided in half. Stage-right half is occupied by* CECILIA's *house. Above this set is another place-name card that reads—"SAN DIMAS". The interior is very simple, 1940s style with a few plants and a "woman's touch" about it. Sofa and chair with coffee table between them. Curtained windows, again looking out into black. Stage-left set is in blackness and should "disappear" as much as possible. Lights up stage right on* CECILIA *in action, serving tea on a tray to* CARTER *who is seated on sofa facing her.* CECILIA *is a very attractive yet slightly eccentric dark-haired woman in her mid-thirties. She wears a brightly flowered Japanese silk robe. Her hair up off her neck but unruly strands are dangling free.*

CECILIA (*serving tea on coffee table*): So, you and Vinnie go back a long way, huh?

CARTER: Yeah, that's right. We do. Clear back to the fifties in fact.

CECILIA: That far?

CARTER: Back to the days of "I LIKE IKE".

CECILIA: That's hard to believe.

CARTER: Why's that?

CECILIA: I don't know. It's hard to believe he's ever known anyone for any length of time. He's such a loner.

CARTER: Well, he wasn't always like that, you know.

CECILIA: Like what?

CARTER: Separate. I mean—remote, like he is.

CECILIA (*offering tea*): Milk and honey?

CARTER: Oh, no thanks. Just black or—whatever you call it.

CECILIA: Tea. I call it tea.

CARTER: Yes. I'm used to drinking coffee, I guess. You know—black coffee. Force of habit.

CECILIA: Oh, I'm sorry. I should have asked. I'm strictly a tea drinker myself. Don't even keep coffee in the house. It gets me rattled.

CARTER: That's all right. This is fine.

CECILIA: Are you sure? I've got hot chocolate if you want. Ovaltine.

CARTER: No. This is great.

CECILIA: I've got little miniature marshmallows.

CARTER: No, really.

*Pause.*

CECILIA: I got into it in London. Back in the seventies.

CARTER: What?

CECILIA: Tea.

CARTER: Oh. I see. But you're not English, are you?

CECILIA: No, no. Missouri. Independence, Missouri. "Home of Harry Truman". "Plain-Talkin' Harry".

CARTER: Right. Independence. Mark Twain's from there too, isn't he?

CECILIA: No, that's Hannibal. Hannibal, Missouri.

CARTER: Oh, that's right! Hannibal. I get them confused.

CECILIA: They just had the flood.

CARTER: Right.

CECILIA: Haven't been back there since I left.

CARTER (*glancing at his watch*): I'll be darned.

CECILIA: I've got no nostalgia about the place. "Americana" bores the shit out of me. Tom Sawyer and Huckleberry Finn. Who are they kidding? I went straight to London and never looked back.

CARTER: Well—That must've been kind of a shock, huh?

CECILIA: It was, but I loved it. London. Sipping tea and reading Byron, you know. I still think of it as home actually.

CARTER: Is that right.

CECILIA: It's the dampness I think. The moisture in the air. Something haunting about it. All that history.

CARTER: Right.

CECILIA: Hounds.

CARTER: What?

CECILIA: Hunting to hounds.

CARTER: Oh, right. Look—Vinnie was wondering—

CECILIA: But you and Vinnie are from around here originally?

CARTER: Yes. Yes, we are as a matter of fact. Only about ten miles away. Cucamonga. Pretty boring. "Home of Grapes".

CECILIA: Grapes?

CARTER: Yeah. Used to be nothing but vineyards as far as the eye could see. Cheap grapes—you know. "Ripple". "Thunderbird". Nothing fancy. Headache wine.

CECILIA: Hard to think of anybody being actually *from* this area.

CARTER: It is, isn't it. But it's true. Born and raised.

CECILIA: You went to school together?

CARTER: Yes, we did. From the sixth grade on.

CECILIA: Sixth grade? So you must have been through a lot then, huh? Lots of ups and downs.

CARTER: We have.

CECILIA: There's something nice about that—Having an on-going friendship. Must give you a real sense of continuity.

CARTER: Well—

CECILIA: I miss that myself.

CARTER: What.

CECILIA: Continuity. Everything seems so busted up to me. Like I've lived a dozen different lives. But a long-lasting friendship—That must be a very nice thing to have.

CARTER: Well—yes and no.

CECILIA: Oh, I suppose there's times when you'd just as soon throw in the towel. Go your separate ways.

CARTER: There are. Yes.

CECILIA: But then you must just see yourself through those rough spots because you realize the value of continuity. "Perseverance Furthers". Remember that?

CARTER: What?

CECILIA: The I-Ching. "Perseverance Furthers". I don't know how many times I used to roll the coins and it came up "Perseverance Furthers". Must've been trying to tell me something, I guess.

CARTER: I don't know uh—anything about that.

CECILIA: Oh, it was just a fad for a while. Everybody used to do it so I did it. I don't do it anymore.

CARTER: What's that?

CECILIA: Roll the coins. It was just a fad. You know—but then there's lots of things that just kind of fall by the wayside as you get older. Don't you think?

CARTER: I guess—I was—

CECILIA: Like cheating on your partner. I gave that up too.

*Pause. She sips tea.*

CARTER: Uh—I wanted to talk to you about Vinnie—

CECILIA: Never used to bother me at all. That's what's so amazing. No guilt. No remorse. No nothing. Then one day it just stopped. Why do you suppose that is?

CARTER: I have no idea.

CECILIA: It had nothing to do with conscience or will-power or anything like that. It just suddenly came to an end. I knew it was over.

CARTER: What.

CECILIA: Cheating.

CARTER (*trying to make a joke out of tension*): Yeah. Remember the days when sex was safe and racing was dangerous?

CARTER *laughs nervously.* CECILIA *doesn't. Pause.*

CECILIA: That's not the reason I stopped.

CARTER: Oh, I didn't mean—You're not with a uh—"partner" now, are you?

CECILIA: Oh, no! Not now. I was talking about the past. The distant past. That's why it was so great meeting up with someone like Vinnie. He kind of reminded me of myself.

CARTER: How's that?

CECILIA: Just the way he was fishing in the dark, I guess. Experimenting.

CARTER: Oh, you mean the "detective" routine? Well see, that's what he wanted me to try to explain to you.

CECILIA: You don't have to explain.

CARTER: No, but see—

CECILIA: I don't need you to explain him to me. In fact I wish you wouldn't. I understand exactly what he's going through.

CARTER: You do?

CECILIA: Yes. Of course.

CARTER: So, you've uh—dropped the charges then, I guess, huh?

CECILIA: What charges? (*Pause.*) Who *are* you exactly?

CARTER: I told you. I'm an old friend of Vinnie's.

CECILIA: Anybody could say that, just to get in the door. Have you been observing me or something? Stalking me?

CARTER: No, look—I'm perfectly legitimate. I have full identification and everything. References if you want. I'm licensed to race in six states.

CECILIA: How can you identify your friendship? How is that possible? Do you have pictures of it or something? The two of you holding hands? Displaying strings of trout?

CARTER: No, I don't carry pictures with me—Look—call him up if you don't believe me. Go ahead and call him. Better yet, we could both go over there and meet him face to face.

CECILIA: You're not getting me in a car alone, buster, if that's what you think. I'm young but I wasn't born yesterday.

CARTER: Whoa! Hang on a second. Let's just slow down here, all right? I have no intention of harming you or molesting you or anything else. Let's be very clear about that.

CECILIA: I suppose you're a detective too, huh? Is that it? Partners in crime?

CARTER: No! I am *not* a detective and neither is Vinnie! That's what I'm trying to get at here. Vinnie is a very sick individual and he needs serious medical attention, in case you didn't know it.

CECILIA: Sick?

CARTER: Well—

CECILIA: He's not a rapist or anything?

CARTER: No. Nothing like that.

CECILIA: I didn't think so. I can usually tell when someone's potentially harmful. I've developed a keen sense of that over the years. I got a sense of you too. Right off the bat. Soon as I saw you through my little window. A man in trouble.

CARTER: *I'm* not in trouble. Vinnie's in trouble.

CECILIA: Soon as I saw you step up on my porch and arch your neck back like you were trying to relieve yourself of serious pain.

CARTER: I came here to talk about my friend, Vinnie! That's the only reason I came. I'm not here to be psychoanalyzed.

CECILIA: As though the pain in your neck was only a symptom of something much bigger. A much bigger pain.

CARTER: Look—I have a plane to catch. I'm only here for a very short time. I would like to keep the conversation on Vinnie, if you don't mind. Do you think that's possible?

CECILIA: I don't see why not. More tea?

CARTER: No, thank you.

*Pause.*

CECILIA: Where are you flying off to?

CARTER: Kentucky.

CECILIA: Aah, my favorite state!

CARTER: Is that right.

CECILIA: "Home of the Derby"!

CARTER: Exactly.

CECILIA: The "Blue Grass State".

CARTER: Yes.

CECILIA: "My Old Kentucky Home"!

CARTER: Look—Could we—

CECILIA: I used to dream about the Derby.

CARTER: Is that a fact.

CECILIA: One of the last bastions of true American aristoc-
racy, don't you think?

CARTER: Yeah, sure.

CECILIA: The closest thing we have to English royalty.
Pomp and circumstance!

CARTER: I don't know.

CECILIA: Have you ever been?

CARTER: Where?

CECILIA: To the Kentucky Derby?

CARTER: Many times.

CECILIA: No, really? And you say it so casually, as though
you've almost become bored with it. I would die to go
to the Derby!

CARTER: It's part of my business.

CECILIA: What business?

CARTER: The horse business. Thoroughbreds.

CECILIA: You're kidding! Vinnie was involved in that too,
wasn't he? A long time ago. Seems like he told me
something about that. Of course it wasn't on the same
scale as the Derby.

CARTER: He may have been. I don't know. Could we please—

CECILIA: You two must have a *lot* in common.

CARTER: We used to.

CECILIA: But now you've drifted. That's too bad. It's sad actually. It's the one thing that breaks my heart.

CARTER: What's that.

CECILIA: People drifting apart. It's worse than death, I think. Worse than dying alone, like a dog. Don't you think?

CARTER: I don't know. I don't know anything about that stuff. All I want to do is just try to explain something to you here and then I'll be on my way. I don't want to take up any more of your time.

CECILIA: I'm not a busy woman. I've got all the time in the world.

CARTER: Fine. That's fine. I'd just like to—I'm not sure you realize exactly how much you mean to Vinnie.

CECILIA: No, I'm sure I don't. We've only known each other a short while.

CARTER: He told me—now this could just be another one of his bizarre delusions—but he told me that you had become a little bit miffed at him over some incident or other. That you had filed certain charges against him. Criminal charges.

CECILIA: Charged him? You mean gone to the police?

CARTER: That's right. That's what he claims. He says he was arrested.

CECILIA: Now why would I do something like that? We were having an affair, for Christ's sake.

CARTER: You were?

CECILIA: Yes. We were. We *are* as far as I'm concerned. Unless he's changed his mind. Is that what this is all about? He couldn't bring himself to face me directly so he sent *you* with the bad news? His old "buddy"?

CARTER: What bad news? No, look—

CECILIA (*standing suddenly*): If it's over, it's over! He doesn't have to send a middleman. Tell him that for *me*!

CARTER: It's *not* over! He wants to see you. He's desperate about it in fact. He called me all the way out here.

CECILIA: Yeah, he's so desperate he's got to send somebody else to take his place!

CARTER: I'm not—He was under the impression that you were pissed off at him!

CECILIA: I *am* pissed off at him!

CARTER: Not *now*! Then!

CECILIA: When?

CARTER: At the time you made the charges against him!

CECILIA: I never made any crumby charges!! I might have called the police but I—

*Pause.*

CARTER: Oh. Then—

CECILIA: Why don't you just get the hell on outa here, mister, and tell your old pal to take a hike for me. Go on! Get outa here!

CARTER (*standing awkwardly*): Now wait a second—Just wait a second. This whole thing has gotten outa hand. I'm very, very sorry if I gave you the wrong idea here. Vinnie's crazy about you. He really is. I've never seen him act this way before. He talks about you like you were sent from heaven or something.

CECILIA: Heaven?

CARTER: Yeah. He said you answered this little prayer of his.

CECILIA: What prayer? Get outa here. This is too weird.

CARTER: All he wants is to see you and talk to you. That's all he wants. He misses you terribly.

CECILIA: Then why doesn't he come over here himself? Why does he send you?

CARTER: He didn't "send" me. I volunteered.

CECILIA: There's something very fishy about this.

CARTER: I guess he thought you weren't going to be very receptive to him. I mean, assuming he was telling the truth.

CECILIA: About what?

CARTER: ABOUT BEING ARRESTED!

*Pause.*

CECILIA: Don't raise your voice in my home, mister.

CARTER: I'm sorry. It's just—that I'm worried about him.

CECILIA: You're worried?

CARTER: I am. I've seen this pattern of his before.

CECILIA: What pattern?

CARTER: This—despair he gets into. This—anguish.

CECILIA: Anguish and despair.

CARTER: It's no joke. He's liable to do something very serious to himself.

CECILIA: Oh. I see.

CARTER: If you could just come with me over there and have a talk with him—

CECILIA: I'm *not* getting into your car, pal. So just give it up.

CARTER: No, I didn't mean that! You can go there any way you want. Walk, drive, take the bus! It makes no difference to me *how* you get there! I just think that it would do him a world of good if he could see you and— talk things out.

*Pause.*

CECILIA: He told you that *I* had him arrested? For what?

CARTER: Trespassing. Invasion of Privacy and uh—Harassment.

CECILIA: That's amazing.

CARTER: He could have been making it all up. It's possible.

CECILIA: I really liked him, you know. Right from the get-go. He seemed like such a sweet man, underneath. Innocent. A man like that has no business being in such a seedy occupation as that. It's bound to pull him down sooner or later.

CARTER: What occupation?

CECILIA: A private investigator. It just doesn't suit him at all.

CARTER: No, see, that's exactly what I'm trying—

CECILIA: He has all kinds of potential, but you can't continue to rub up against that kind of low-rent world he lives in without feeling the effects.

CARTER: He is *not* a private investigator! He's not a detective or anything like that! That's what I've been trying to get through to you, here!

CECILIA: He showed me his badge and his gun. He took me on surveillance with him. He even showed me pictures from a case he'd worked on.

*Pause.*

CARTER: What case?

CECILIA: Some case involving a racing official or something. He said it was years ago.

CARTER: He talked to you about that?

CECILIA: He talks to me about everything.

CARTER: What'd he tell you?

CECILIA: I can't remember all the details of it. But he wasn't lying.

CARTER: He lies about everything! It's all part of this illness of his. This sickness! He's a professional liar.

CECILIA: Well, the pictures didn't lie. I can tell you that much.

CARTER: What pictures?

CECILIA: He showed me a couple of pictures of this guy that were presented as evidence against him.

CARTER: What were the pictures of?

CECILIA: What difference does it make to you?

CARTER: I am trying to figure out what's going on in his head. That's all.

CECILIA: They were very, very filthy pictures. That's about all I can say. I've never seen anything like it, in fact.

And, believe me, I've been around the block. I may not look it but I have.

CARTER: Was there a woman involved?

CECILIA: A woman?

CARTER: In the pictures!

CECILIA: What's your interest in this, anyway?

CARTER: Let me see them.

CECILIA: What?

CARTER: THE PICTURES! THE PHOTOGRAPHS! Do you still have them?

*Pause.*

CECILIA: You're a very strange man, mister. You don't come into somebody's home, a total stranger, and start raising your voice and making demands. Where were you brought up?

CARTER: I'm sorry.

CECILIA: I don't care who you are but you don't start acting like a cop in my own house. Unless you are a cop?

CARTER: I'm *not* a cop. I'm not a detective. I'm just worried about my friend, that's all. This business with the pictures is quite a surprise. I mean if he's actually gone so far as to set somebody up—or put someone's personal integrity in jeopardy then—well, he's in trouble. Big trouble. I don't know if I can bail him out of this kind of a mess.

CECILIA: Someone's personal integrity?

CARTER: Yes, that's right.

CECILIA: He told me this case happened years ago.

CARTER: It doesn't matter!

CECILIA: He said everything about the case had probably been long forgotten.

CARTER: Something like that is never forgotten! Never. Believe me. It could loom its ugly head at any given moment and destroy an innocent man's life.

CECILIA: Well he couldn't have been all *that* innocent. This commissioner guy. Some of those postures I've never seen in the animal kingdom.

CARTER: Let me see them.

CECILIA: I didn't save them or anything. I'm not a pervert.

CARTER: What'd you do with them?

CECILIA: I don't have a clue. I might have given them back to Vinnie.

CARTER: He said *you* had them! Did you destroy them?

CECILIA: No.

CARTER: Did you let them out of the house?

*Pause.*

CECILIA: Oh. So he already told you about it then?

CARTER: What?

CECILIA: The pictures. You already know.

CARTER: He mentioned something—

CECILIA: So why are you acting so surprised?

CARTER: Look, I can't stress how important it is to locate these photographs. Vinnie could go to jail for a very long time.

CECILIA: Vinnie could?

CARTER: Yes. He could. He certainly could. I mean—I'm just trying to keep him out of trouble. That's all I've been doing for the last fifteen years.

*Pause.* CARTER *moves to window and stares out as* CECILIA *watches him.*

CARTER: There's a lot of other things I'd rather have been doing. Believe me. I'm a busy man but—I figured I owed it to Vinnie. He just never seemed to get the same breaks, you know. So—Anyhow, I thought I'd just make a quick trip out here and get him fixed up. You know—whatever he needed—and then get right back home. It's always been like that in the past. I've always taken care of him. And I don't mind. I mean—I figured I kinda owed it to him, you know. It's my responsibility. I can't just—get rid of him. (*Pause, checks his watch.*) Shit, I've already missed my flight I think. (*Turns to* CECILIA.) Look, would you just consider meeting me over there at his place—in an hour or so. Please, just consider it. We could get all this straightened out. It would do him a world of good. We could all get back to normal.

*Pause. She stares at him.*

CECILIA: More tea?

*She pours as lights dim into cross-fade.*

## SCENE TWO

*Night. Place-name card above stage-left set reads—"MIDWAY. KY. 'RED EYE' ". Cross-fade. Lights up on* SIMMS' *bloodstock office in Kentucky.* SIMMS *is bent over his desk, absorbed in paperwork, surrounded by reference books, stacks of magazines, etc. A small window directly behind him, looking out into blackness. A leather armchair in faded green across from* SIMMS' *desk. Racing pictures and genealogy charts on walls.* SIMMS, *in his mid-sixties, wears a grey vest over a white shirt with sleeves rolled up. Dark slacks. Everything rumpled and worn. A green visor-cap to shade his eyes from the overhead lamp.* VINNIE *enters out of darkness left with a "Redwing" shoebox tucked under his arm.* SIMMS *continues his paperwork, oblivious. Pause.*

VINNIE: Uh—Mr Ames? Ryan Ames?

SIMMS: What'd they do, leave the hallway unlocked? Man could be murdered this time a' night.

VINNIE: I'm sorry. The door was open. I'm Vincent Webb. Vincent T. Webb. From California.

> VINNIE *crosses to desk.* SIMMS *remains seated. They shake hands across desk.*

SIMMS: Vincent T. Webb.

VINNIE: Sorry to interrupt—

SIMMS: Nothin' to it. Just the usual obsessive perusal of charts: Sire lists; auction reports. Can't study enough on the Blood Horse these days.

VINNIE: No, I suppose not.

SIMMS: Most boys have all this modern software nonsense— computer read-outs and what-have-you. Fax machines. Electronic mail. Me, I still prefer to stumble around with the old-fashioned dirty paper. I like to fondle it. Gives me a feeble sense of something tangible in the midst of all the abstract frenzy.

VINNIE: Yeah. I know what you mean.

SIMMS: So, you're a Western man, huh? Out in the Golden Land of high purses and racial conflict?

VINNIE: That's right.

SIMMS: Still run *live* horse racing out there, do ya, or is it all on the TV monitor now like it is across the rest of wide America?

VINNIE: Oh no, they uh—still have live racing. They sure do. Santa Anita. Del Mar. You know—they're institutions.

SIMMS: "Off-Track Betting"! Who invented that one?

VINNIE: I'm not sure.

SIMMS: Bandits! Bandits and cuff-snappers. You don't belong to either of those two sub-species, do you?

VINNIE: No, sir. I'm—

SIMMS: Bushwhackers and Backstabbers. Snakes. Whole damn industry's full a' snakes now. Thoroughbred's gonna be an obsolete animal before you know it. They'll find some way to turn the whole damn thing into a Pac-Man Game. You wait and see.

VINNIE: I suppose so.

SIMMS: No question about it. All the icons are dead and buried—"Sonny-Jim" Fitzsimmons, "Bull" Hancock, Mr Madden—This is the very last generation of honest-to-God true horsemen. Once they're gone, the game's up.

VINNIE: That'll be a sad day in hell, won't it.

SIMMS: You got that right. (*Pause.*) What line a' work do you follow, Mr Webb?

VINNIE: Uh—well I—I dabble somewhat. I mean—

SIMMS: A dabbler! Good thing to be. Little a' this, little a' that. Not enough "dabblers" these days, I'd say. Too many experts.

VINNIE: Well—I don't know.

SIMMS: In what area do you do the most "dabbling", Mr Webb?

VINNIE: Well, I—fool around with pedigrees and—

SIMMS: A pedigree man! There ya go. My line exactly.

VINNIE: But only as a sideline.

SIMMS: Aha.

VINNIE: A hobby—kind of.

SIMMS: A hobby.

VINNIE: I used to be very involved—I mean I was in the horse business some time ago. I've kinda—lost touch.

SIMMS: Helps to keep abreast of things, that's for sure. A stallion can move up and down the lists in a matter of days. Requires constant scrutiny. That is, if you want to stay in the game.

VINNIE: Yeah, I can see where it would.

SIMMS: Used to be no such a thing as a "bloodstock agent". Now you've got owners dumber than dirt. Don't know "Native Dancer" from "Nasrullah". Couldn't tell a sesamoid from a cannon-bone and couldn't care less about it.

VINNIE: Yeah—

SIMMS: So what's your main line, Mr Webb?

VINNIE: Excuse me?

SIMMS: You said pedigrees was a sideline. What's your *main* line?

VINNIE: Oh, uh—well, actually I've been working as a private investigator for the past five years.

SIMMS: A "sleuth"! A "gumshoe", as we used to call 'em.

VINNIE: That's right.

SIMMS: How 'bout that. Used to love those old detective movies. Raymond Chandler. Dashiell Hammett. Don't make enough a' those kinda movies anymore, do they?

VINNIE: No, they sure don't.

SIMMS: Don't make *any* of 'em, as a matter of fact.

VINNIE: I guess not.

SIMMS: *Double Indemnity*, *Maltese Falcon*. Pictures with a plot you could sink your teeth into.

VINNIE: Right.

SIMMS: Who was it decided to do away with all the plots?

VINNIE: What?

SIMMS: They must've had a meeting somewhere. Behind closed doors.

VINNIE: I don't know. I—stopped going to the movies.

SIMMS: Wise decision, Mr Webb. Very wise. (*Pause.*) So— you're an authentic detective, is that it?

VINNIE: It's—a way to make a living.

SIMMS: Must come across some dyed-in-the-wool characters, in the course of things.

VINNIE: Yeah. You do. You sure do.

SIMMS: Some real scumbags too, I suppose.

VINNIE: Yup. Plenty of those.

SIMMS: So, what do you need from me? All the low-down on somebody's sleazy past? Oh, I've seen 'em all roll through this little murky office, believe you me. The whole wide spectrum.

VINNIE: I'll bet you have.

SIMMS: It's the spotless ones you gotta watch out for. The "lawyer-types". The ones who've got beepers hung on their hips and tassled loafers free of manure. They can't go to the bathroom without carrying their carphones with 'em. They're the ones who'll kill a horse to collect the insurance. Pay a groom to cut their air off in the middle of the night. Ruthless and clean as a whistle.

VINNIE: No, uh—I'm actually on a search for a man who used to hold a very high position out West.

SIMMS: Oh, I see. A kingpin, huh?

VINNIE: A man—who fell from grace.

SIMMS: Well, that includes just about everybody on my Christmas card list, Mr Webb. Have a seat.

VINNIE: "Vinnie". You can call me "Vinnie".

VINNIE *sits in armchair as* SIMMS *gets up, moves to a liquor cabinet tucked into bookshelves, takes out a bottle of bourbon and glasses.*

SIMMS: "Vinnie"? Sounds more New Jersey than California.

VINNIE: Yeah. I know. Friends always called me "Vinnie". Short for Vincent, you know—

SIMMS: Bourbon, Vinnie?

VINNIE: Uh—no thanks.

SIMMS: *Kentucky* bourbon? Maker's Mark, Fighting Cock?

VINNIE: No. That's all right. I'm on the wagon.

SIMMS: Yeah, I was on that for a while myself but the wheels broke off. (*Pours himself a drink.*) So—you're on a manhunt, is that it?

VINNIE: More, less. I happened to accidentally come across some material in the course of an entirely different investigation. This uh—material was so shocking, in a way, that I got sidetracked.

SIMMS: I see. And what type of "material" would that be?

VINNIE: Well, it was of a pornographic nature.

SIMMS: Aha! Pornographic! Now we're talkin' modern language. It's just about all pornographic these days, isn't it, Mr Webb? Not much left that isn't.

VINNIE: Well, I suppose. If you look at it that way.

SIMMS: That's exactly the way I look at it. Music, news, politics—pornography personified. Wouldn't you say?

VINNIE: Um—This stuff I came across is so specifically amoral that, unfortunately, it became incriminating to the party in question.

SIMMS: So, he must've paid the piper then, huh? This "party"?

VINNIE: Yes. He did.

SIMMS: Probably paid ten times over. Didn't he?

VINNIE: Well—

SIMMS: Must've suffered very dearly for his little transgression. Maybe suffered far more than any of his revilers could've imagined. That's the way it usually goes.

VINNIE: I don't know.

SIMMS: No. Of course not. How could you? You'd have to be inside the man's skin, wouldn't you?

*Pause.*

VINNIE: My point is—What I'm trying to get at, is that I've uncovered some very interesting evidence along with this material.

SIMMS: And what would that be?

VINNIE: Well, on closer examination and following a few crazy leads that I had, it would appear that this man was framed.

SIMMS: Is that right? And what led you to that conclusion, Mr Webb?

VINNIE: Well, I started to delve into it a little bit and—

SIMMS: "Dabble."

VINNIE: Excuse me?

SIMMS: Never mind. You started to "delve" and . . . ?

VINNIE: Yes. I traced the photographs right back to their source. There were dates on the negatives, see—

SIMMS: Photographs?

VINNIE: Right. That's the "material" I was referring to.

SIMMS: I see.

VINNIE: I've got them right here.

SIMMS: In the shoebox.

VINNIE: Yes. I've got all of them. The negatives.

SIMMS: The originals.

VINNIE: That's right.

SIMMS: Dirty pictures.

VINNIE: They are. No question about it.

SIMMS: Are you a Puritan, Mr Webb?

VINNIE: Am I—what?

SIMMS: A Puritan. A "Founding Father"?

VINNIE: No, I—

SIMMS: Does sex trouble you?

VINNIE: No. I've got no problem with that.

SIMMS: Are you terrified by a beautiful woman?

VINNIE: No!

SIMMS: You indulge in the odd blow-job from time to time?

VINNIE: What? Look—

SIMMS: No?

VINNIE: I'm not here to—

SIMMS: Never?

VINNIE: Maybe once—or twice—in the past.

SIMMS: In the past?

VINNIE: A long time ago. I can't remember. A long, long time ago.

SIMMS: Did you enjoy it?

VINNIE: What?

SIMMS: The blow-job in the past. Did you enjoy it?

VINNIE: I can't remember. I was very, very young—

SIMMS: Did you wish it would last forever or did you just take it in your stride, like a man, and go on about your business? Go on "living your life", as they say? Realizing there's no such thing as eternal ecstasy?

VINNIE: I'm trying to explain something here!

SIMMS: That you were shocked.

VINNIE: No! I mean about the origin of the photographs!

SIMMS: You are shocked even though you yourself had debauched in the very same activity. Probably worse.

VINNIE: Worse?

SIMMS: No?

VINNIE: No. Never like this stuff. I mean this is really—

SIMMS: Really what?

VINNIE: Barbaric. I mean—Primitive.

*Pause.*

SIMMS: I see. Barbaric. Carries an edge of violence, does it?

VINNIE: What I'm trying to say is that—this man was set up and I happen to know the party responsible. I have letters. Correspondence. Absolute proof.

*Pause.*

SIMMS: How many lives do you think a man can live, Mr Webb? How many lives within this *one*?

VINNIE: I'm not sure I understand you, sir.

SIMMS: Well, say for instance, you could put the past to death and start over. Right now. You look like you might be a candidate for that.

VINNIE: That's not possible. I mean—

SIMMS: No? Vengeance appeals to you more.

VINNIE: Vengeance?

SIMMS: Yes. Blood. Now why is that? Why is blood more appealing than re-birth? Is it the color? The satisfaction of seeing it out in the open? Bursting free of its fleshy boundaries?

VINNIE: I'm not—I'm just trying to help out an innocent man, that's all.

SIMMS: Ah, so it's *innocence* that attracts you! Justice!

VINNIE: I'm a detective! That's my job. I'm paid to get to the bottom of things.

SIMMS: And who's paying you now?

VINNIE: Well, that's the thing—I've struck out on my own because I believe I could help this condemned man reinstate himself.

SIMMS: Vindication!

VINNIE: Yes. Exactly.

SIMMS: And he would, most likely, be very grateful for that. This poor man. This fallen soul. Most likely he would pay you a great deal of money.

VINNIE: I'm not interested in money.

SIMMS: No?

VINNIE: No.

SIMMS: Did you know this sinner? Is he a personal friend of yours?

VINNIE: No, he's not.

SIMMS: Then it *is* blood. Am I right?

VINNIE: Not exactly.

SIMMS: Well, if it's not blood or money then it must be drugs or sex.

VINNIE: No. It's not any of that.

SIMMS: Don't tell me you're a man of honor? The last of a dying breed? Is that possible, Mr Webb?

VINNIE: The man I'm looking for went under the name of "Simms". "Darrel P. Simms". Does that ring any kind of a bell with you, Mr "Ames"?

*Pause.*

SIMMS: "Simms"? "Darrel P." Nope. Can't say that it does.

VINNIE: Commissioner of Racing in Southern California, nineteen fifty-nine through seventy-eight. Approximately.

SIMMS: Ah! California. Now that's a whole different ball-park. Tough for us old Kentucky Hardboots to keep pace with the West Coast, ya know. Hard for us to consider it legitimate when we're straddling the apex right here.

VINNIE: You're not from Kentucky originally though, are you?

SIMMS: Bourbon County. Born and bred.

VINNIE: Oh. I didn't realize that.

SIMMS: No. How could you? You don't know me from Adam. Do you, Mr Webb?

*Pause.*

VINNIE: If I could find this man—If you could help me track him down, I'm sure he'd be very interested in what I've uncovered.

SIMMS: Why are you so sure?

VINNIE: He can't help but be interested! He's been living in the shadow of blackmail now for fifteen years! Look—there's a very powerful figure here, in the racing industry, who's gotten away with murder at Mr Simms' expense.

SIMMS: I'm not in the muckraking business, Mr Webb. I'm in the horse business. You're either buying gold or mining for gold but you'll never find a diamond up a goat's ass. I don't give two shits about these festering souls and all their dirty laundry. I'm obsessed with my work. Can you understand that?

VINNIE: Yes, but I have *inside* information—

SIMMS: I'm so completely absorbed in my work that the outside world has disappeared. It's vanished, Mr Webb. I'm no longer seduced by its moaning and fanfare. I'm busy with the "Sport of Kings"

VINNIE: But I could turn this whole thing around for Simms! He could be completely exonerated and Carter would end up crawling on his knees like a lizard.

SIMMS: Carter? Lyle Carter?

*Pause.*

VINNIE: Yes. That's right.

SIMMS: You're kinda plowin' in high cotton, aren't ya boy? You need to go see the powers that be. I'm just a little ole bloodstock agent. That's all I am. Seasons and shares. Small potatoes. And I like it that way.

VINNIE: But you—

SIMMS: What?

VINNIE: You must have heard of this man, "Simms", somewhere along the line. I mean—over the years.

SIMMS: As a matter of fact, I *did* hear of him. Quite a while back. Out West somewhere. I suppose it could've been California. I think maybe you're right about that.

Vilified in the press, as I remember. Slandered. Railroaded outa town.

VINNIE: That's him! It was all over the news.

SIMMS: They had a field-day.

VINNIE: That's the man!

SIMMS: Lost his family too, I believe.

*Pause.*

VINNIE: Oh. I didn't know that.

SIMMS: Yes. Wife and kids packed it up on him. I believe that's right. Bankrupt. Lost everything in fact. Bottomed out completely.

VINNIE: I'm sorry to hear that.

SIMMS: Why should you be sorry? Loss can be a powerful elixir.

VINNIE: I mean—in general. It's uh—a sad thing.

SIMMS: That's just something to say, Mr Webb. That's just something lame to say.

VINNIE: Yes, but—

SIMMS: You have no way of knowing. Do you?

VINNIE: No—but—What became of him?

SIMMS: "Simms"? Disappeared I think.

VINNIE: He never showed up under a pseudonym—an alias of some kind?

SIMMS: Not to my knowledge, no. 'Course you're free to snoop around town. Do your "dabbling". After all, gossip happens to be Lexington's second biggest industry. My guess though, if you *do* happen to find him, is that he's willing to let sleeping dogs lay. That's just my hunch.

VINNIE: Why would you suppose that? He's got everything to gain.

SIMMS: I'm a gambler, Mr Webb. We go on hunches.

VINNIE: But if I was him—if I was this man and I had this kind of an opportunity—to come out of hiding—to live out in the open again and regain my—my self-esteem— my good standing in the public eye—To move freely. It just seems to me—

SIMMS: You're not.

VINNIE: What?

SIMMS: You're *not* this man.

*Lights dim into cross-fade.*


## SCENE THREE

*Night. Cross-fade back to stage-right split set. Place-name card above reads—"CUCAMONGA". Lights up on* VINNIE's *room from Act One.* CARTER *is sitting on bed, sifting through contents of cardboard boxes he's pulled out from underneath* VINNIE's *bed: letters, photographs etc. and* VINNIE's *detective paraphernalia.* CARTER *in shirtsleeves now with cuffs rolled up, collar open, tie hanging loose. He drinks from* VINNIE's *bottle. His suit jacket and overcoat are thrown on foot of bed. His briefcase containing cellular phone is on the floor, center stage.* CECILIA *moves through the room, pausing at dirty dishes and* VINNIE's *pile of dirty laundry.*

CECILIA (*examining laundry*): I can't believe he lives like this. Gives you a whole different impression of someone when you see how they actually live.

CARTER: Yes, it does doesn't it. He's basically a pig.

CECILIA: Well, I wouldn't go that far.

CARTER: He's always been a pig.

CECILIA: It's just so stark and—

CARTER: I told him he needed a few throw-rugs to liven the place up, but he wouldn't listen.

CECILIA: Do you think you ought to be going through his private things like that? I mean, what if you come across something personal?

CARTER: I'll ignore it.

*Pause. She moves to the sink as* CARTER *keeps sorting through papers, etc.*

CECILIA: Look at these dishes! There's ants all over the place. Trails of ants.

CARTER: You don't have any idea where he may have stashed them, do you? The photographs?

CECILIA *begins rinsing dishes and washing them as* CARTER *continues.*

CECILIA: No, I never ask him things like that. It's none of my business.

CARTER: I thought you and him were having some big flaming affair.

CECILIA: Well, I don't know how big and flaming it was— but I don't pry into his private life.

CARTER: So, you've never even been in this place, evidently?

CECILIA (*washing dishes*): No. I never have.

CARTER: So all the uh—"trysting" must've been done at *your* house, huh?

CECILIA: Trysting?

CARTER: Screwing around. Heavy petting.

CECILIA: We never did that.

CARTER: Oh.

CECILIA: He comes over to my place and we have tea and talk.

CARTER: Tea and talk. Sounds great.

CECILIA: It was. It—*is*.

CARTER: He enthralled you with detective trivia, I suppose.

CECILIA: I was interested in his latest case.

CARTER (*drinking*): Oh yeah? Which one was that? The time he almost toppled the Heads of IT&T?

CECILIA: It was a divorce settlement.

CARTER: Ah! Juicy.

CECILIA: We were working on it together. In fact, it might've been *that* woman who had him arrested. I'll bet it was.

CARTER: I see. Some *other* woman.

CECILIA: She might've felt we were getting too close to the heart of the matter.

CARTER: Poor thing.

CECILIA: It was very exciting. I'd never been on surveillance before.

CARTER: It never occurred to you that the whole deal might be an elaborate game to get you in the sack?

CECILIA: I've told you, we never did that.

CARTER: Never kissed? Never hugged even?

CECILIA *turns to him at the sink.*

CARTER: Just a little peck on the neck?

CECILIA: What's it to you?

CARTER: Just curious.

*Pause.* CECILIA *resumes washing dishes.*

CECILIA: So, where's he gone to? Your best friend. You said he was going to be here. He was "dying to see me".

CARTER: Probably down at the mall or hiking to Glendora. He takes long walks these days. Long, aimless walks.

CECILIA: You make him sound so desperate.

CARTER: Well, there's nothing like heartbreak to drive a man insane. He didn't have that far to go anyway.

CECILIA: He's not crazy. Just lonesome.

CARTER: He's a madman. Didn't you recognize that? Couldn't you see that in his eyeballs when you first slid up next to him at the bar?

CECILIA: What bar?

CARTER: Wherever you met him!

CECILIA: I don't drink.

CARTER: No, of course not! You're a teatotaller.

CECILIA: I met him at the Safeway. That's where I work. I was bagging groceries for him and—

CARTER: Fine! It doesn't matter *where* you met him. My point is that he's nuts! Anyone with half a brain could figure that one out. He's a lunatic!

CECILIA: So now you've suddenly shifted to insults. Is this a tactic of yours or are you just a grumpy drunk?

CARTER: I'm not drunk! I'll let you know when I'm drunk.

CECILIA: That's considerate of you.

CARTER: I just don't see how it's possible for a full-grown woman to fall for that kind of lame, adolescent bullshit. I mean I used to pretend I was the Lone Ranger but I grew out of it.

CECILIA: Did you wear a mask?

CARTER: What?

CECILIA: When you were the Lone Ranger—did you wear a mask?

CARTER: I didn't say I *was* the Lone Ranger, I said I was *pretending* to be the Lone Ranger.

CECILIA: Did you wear a mask?

CARTER: No! I didn't wear a mask! I didn't *need* a mask!

CECILIA: You were that good?

CARTER: Yes! I was.

CECILIA: Did you pull the wool over everyone's eyes?

CARTER: What?

CECILIA: You and Vinnie—the "Detective" and the "Lone Ranger". Did you fool everyone or just each other?

CARTER: Look—"Miss Priss"—Did he ever talk to you about these photographs? Did he ever mention where he might have hid them?

CECILIA: I don't think they were as vital to him as they are to you. The only reason he showed them to me was to share something about his past.

CARTER: Sure.

CECILIA: What?

CARTER: You don't actually believe that, do you? A man shows you a bunch of obscene pictures in order to "share something about his past"? Are you kidding?

CECILIA: He showed them to me as examples of his work. That's all.

CARTER: Why are you so thick, Cecilia? Missouri's raised some very shrewd citizens over the decades. Why aren't you one of them?

CECILIA: You must be quite ruthless in business too, I suppose.

CARTER: Oh yeah, I'm a regular cut-throat.

CARTER's *cellular phone starts buzzing, inside his briefcase. Pause. They both stare at the briefcase.*

CECILIA: Your briefcase is buzzing.

CARTER *stands up and staggers slightly from the booze, then pulls himself together and moves to the briefcase. He stands over it and stares at it. Pause.*

CECILIA: Maybe it's your buddy.

CARTER *squats down, opens briefcase and answers phone. As he does this, lights come up in a dim pool on* SIMMS, *seated at his desk, on the phone, stage left. No card.*

CARTER (*on phone*): Yeah.

SIMMS (*on phone, stage left*): We've got a little problem here, Carter.

CARTER: Who is this?

CARTER *stands slowly.* CECILIA *continues with dishes.*

SIMMS: "Ames". Your man in the Blue Grass.

CARTER: What're you doing calling me here!

SIMMS: Seems your boy has jumped clean across the line. State lines, to be exact.

CARTER: What boy? I've told you never to try to get ahold of me! How'd you get this number?

SIMMS: Your boy, "Vincent T. Webb". He's peddling some very classified material here. Thought you might be interested.

CARTER: What material? What're you talking about? He's out *here!* I just saw him!

SIMMS: Well, he's got a very convincing double then.

CARTER: He came to you?

SIMMS: In the flesh.

CARTER: What's he want?

SIMMS: Three guesses.

CARTER: Don't try to pull anything on me, Simms!

SIMMS: I just thought maybe you'd like to know what's on the open market. I might be able to sell you a share.

SIMMS *hangs up softly. Lights dim on him.* CARTER *stays on phone.*

CARTER: SIMMS! HEY! HELLO! SIMMS! (*He slams phone back into briefcase.*) Lousy, goddamn scummy bastard!

CARTER *moves back to bottle and drinks.*

CECILIA (*at sink*): Who was it?

CARTER: Just—a client. Business.

CECILIA: Simms?

CARTER: What?

CECILIA: Who's Simms?

CARTER: Why don't you just leave now. There's no point in you being here anymore. Vinnie's not here and—

CECILIA: He might come back.

CARTER: He's *not* coming back!

CECILIA: He skipped town?

CARTER: Yes! That's exactly what he did. He skipped town.

CECILIA: Something to do with these photographs?

CARTER: None of this is any of your business! The only reason you're here is because I thought you could bring Vinnie out of this slump he was in.

CECILIA: But now he's run off.

CARTER: That's right.

CECILIA: With all your dirty pictures.

CARTER: They're not *my* dirty pictures!

CECILIA: But you want them. You want them very badly.

CARTER: Will you please leave! Will you go now? Get lost! Vamoose.

CECILIA: You were so eager to get me here. Now you want me gone. It's very confusing.

CARTER *moves back to briefcase, takes phone out and dials.*

CARTER (*as he deals with phone*): I've got things to arrange here. I've already missed my plane. I'm supposed to be back with my family, getting the kids ready for school. Buying notebooks and lunchpails. Halloween's coming up. Little League. There's—

CARTER *listens on phone. As it begins to ring in* SIMMS' *office, lights come up softly on* SIMMS *again, seated at his desk, hovering over his work.* SIMMS *looks at the phone ringing on his desk but doesn't answer. He goes back to his work and lets it ring.*

CECILIA: Little League?

CECILIA *finishes dishes, then moves to* VINNIE's *dirty laundry and starts gathering it up.*

CECILIA: I thought it was football.

CARTER (*still waiting on phone*): Answer the phone, you slimy shithead! ANSWER THE GODDAMN PHONE!!

CARTER *slams the phone back into the briefcase.*

CECILIA (*gathering laundry*): Nobody home?

*Pause.* CARTER *watches her.*

CARTER: What're you doing?

CECILIA: Laundry.

CARTER: Leave it? He doesn't deserve clean laundry. You're not his maid. Just leave it and get out of here.

CECILIA: Little League?

CARTER: What?

CECILIA: Little League in the Fall?

CARTER: I was thinking about the future!

CECILIA: I thought it was football in the Fall.

CARTER: I am *not* in the mood for domestic chit-chat about sports right now! Thank you very much. I'm in the midst of a crisis, in case you didn't notice. Suddenly I'm in the midst of a crisis!

CECILIA: That's the thing about crisis.

CARTER: What?

CECILIA: It happens suddenly.

CARTER: Will you please get the hell out of here!

CECILIA (*continuing to gather laundry*): I'm waiting for Vinnie.

CARTER: Vinnie is *gone*! Understand? He's double-crossed me. Sold me out! Down the river!

CECILIA: That's no way to talk about your best and oldest friend.

CARTER: Vinnie is a weasel! He's a low-down, treacherous, diabolical little man. The scum of the earth. He's systematically trying to crucify me!

CECILIA: For what?

CARTER: Exactly! For what? For something deeply buried in his sick imagination. That's "for what".

CECILIA: What could that be?

CARTER: Excuse me?

CECILIA: Deeply buried?

CARTER: I AM TRYING TO THINK HERE! I AM TRYING TO THINK!!

*Pause.* CARTER *drinks and wanders.* CECILIA *collects laundry.*

CECILIA: Maybe it's a woman.

CARTER: Will you get out! What in the world is the matter with you? You're like a termite or something, boring away. Why do you persist in staying when you know you're not welcome?

CECILIA: You invited me.

CARTER: I know that!

CECILIA: Sometimes, if you just lay all your cards on the table, miraculous things begin to occur. Things you could never foresee.

CARTER: I don't need any half-baked philosophical notions from you. Things are falling apart! THE SKY IS FALLING! THE SKY IS FALLING!

*Pause.* CECILIA *stares at him.*

CECILIA: "Chicken Little", isn't it?

CARTER: Look, smart ass!

CECILIA: You shouldn't be so hard on Vinnie, just because he's a detective and you're not.

CARTER: He's *not* a detective!

CECILIA: Where is he now?

CARTER: Kentucky! He's in Kentucky!

CECILIA: That was fast.

CARTER: He couldn't wait to double-cross me.

CECILIA: That's where you're from.

CARTER: Brilliant.

CECILIA: Are you going back out there? Track him down?

CARTER: I just came from there!

CECILIA: "What goes around, comes around." You ever heard that one? A musician I knew used to say that all the time.

CARTER: I am going to hit you in a minute. I am going to strike you!

CECILIA: You're not on the verge of a nervous breakdown, are you, Mr Carter?

CARTER: I'm being squeezed! Do you know what that's like? Have you got any idea what that's like? It's almost as though he's planned it or something. Set me up. (*Pause.*) You're not in on this with him, are you? The two of you in cahoots?

CECILIA: Vinnie's mind doesn't work like that.

CARTER: His mind? Now we're going to talk about his mind? He *has* no mind! He's brainless!

CECILIA: You're just jealous is all.

CARTER: Jealous?

CECILIA: I think so. There's that tone about it.

CARTER: A jealous tone.

CECILIA: Yes.

CARTER: What is it, exactly, that you find so fascinating about him? It's unbelievable. I mean, I don't get it. You're not a half bad-looking woman, Cecilia.

CECILIA: Gee, thanks.

CARTER: No, I mean really—You're a very attractive young lady, in your own way. It would seem to me that you'd have a lot bigger fish to fry than some down-and-out loser with a detective complex.

CECILIA: Maybe you should lie down.

CARTER: I'm not lying down!

CECILIA: You might be able to think better.

CARTER: I am *not* lying down! I'm not playing into your hand. That's it, isn't it? You get me into the sack and keep me here, while he goes off to knife me in the back.

CECILIA: I'm not a slut Mr Carter.

CARTER: I didn't say that.

CECILIA: Those might be the kind of women you've dealt with in the past but I'm not one of them.

CARTER: What women?

CECILIA: Any woman.

CARTER: Did Vinnie talk to you about women in the past?

CECILIA: Don't get paranoid on me, Mr Carter. Panic is a terrible thing. It's in the air. But there's no reason to succumb to it.

CARTER: I'm not panicked!

CECILIA: I've known panic, myself. You can pick it up from the TV, radio. The telephone. It's like a disease.

CARTER: I AM *NOT* PANICKED!!

CECILIA: It can take over your whole body. Your mind. This sense of impending doom.

*Pause. He stares at her.*

CARTER: You've felt that kind of thing before? Why would you feel something like that? Someone like you. Working in the Safeway. What do you know about "impending doom"? You've never—*done* anything have you? I mean—

CECILIA: Done anything? Like what?

CARTER: Nothing.

CECILIA: No—like what, for instance? I've done lots of things you might never suspect me of.

CARTER: Betrayed—something. Someone.

CECILIA: Oh—Betrayed. I don't know about that. Have you?

CARTER: What?

CECILIA: Betrayed someone?

CARTER: No.

CECILIA: Well, there you are then—both of us must be completely innocent on that score and yet we've both felt impending doom. Isn't that something.

CARTER: Well, maybe not *completely* innocent—

CECILIA: No. Maybe not.

CARTER: I mean little things, here and there. Things that couldn't be helped.

CECILIA: Right.

CARTER: Things—beyond your control.

CECILIA: Well, those things you can't blame yourself for.

CARTER: No.

CECILIA: Those things are just—

CARTER: Accidental, almost.

CECILIA: That's right.

CARTER: Circumstance.

*Pause.* CARTER *stares at her.*

CARTER: How did he find you exactly? He just strolled into the Safeway one day and there you were—bagging his groceries?

CECILIA: Coincidence, I guess.

CARTER: And he never even kissed you? Never tried? I—I don't understand that.

CECILIA: He kissed me once.

*Pause.*

CARTER: He did?

CECILIA: Yes. Just once.

CARTER: Where?

CECILIA: In my kitchen.

CARTER: I mean on your body! Where on your body!

*Pause.*

CECILIA: That's private, Mr Carter.

*Pause.*

CARTER: I'm going to lay down.

CECILIA: Yes. I think you should.

CARTER *goes to bed, takes a long drink of whiskey and lies down.*

CARTER: I have no idea what to do now. I can't go back there, I can't stay here. I can't—face it. I can't—It's like everything's going backwards! I came out here to fix things up! Why is he doing this to me?

CECILIA: Would you like a neck rub?

CARTER: No! Don't touch me!

CECILIA: You should try to rest now.

CARTER: I *am* resting! I'm supposed to be home but I'm resting. I'm supposed to be taking care of business! I'm the backbone of the whole operation and I'm laying here in Vinnie's bed.

CECILIA: Just breathe softly through your nose. Try to relax.

CARTER: Don't tell me how to breathe! I know how to breathe.

CECILIA: You'll be all right.

CARTER: Why did you let him kiss you! Why'd you let him do that?

CECILIA: Mr Carter—

*She reaches out and touches his back softly.* CARTER *jerks up and sits on bed.*

CARTER: DON'T TOUCH ME!

CECILIA *backs off.*

CECILIA: All right. Take it easy. I was just going to—

CARTER: He wants me to crawl, see. That's what it is. He wants me to suffer. It's not enough that I pay through the nose—that I cater to each and every little need of his—that I send him T-shirts and socks and see that all his bills are paid—HE WANTS ME TO SUFFER!! It's a vendetta!

CARTER *takes another belt from the bottle, gets up and starts to move through the room.*

CECILIA: You should really try to calm yourself down. It's not good for your blood.

CARTER (*on the move*): He was the one, see—That's what everybody forgets. He was the one with the big ideas. Right from the get-go. "All we'll do is switch a couple a' racehorses. That's all." That's what he said. "Happens all the time. Nobody'll know. They're both bay. Both geldings. Two white socks. Doctor the lip tattoos.

They're identical. Who's gonna know? Public always loses anyway!" That's what he said. "The track's robbing them ten times worse than we are. It's not like it's murder or rape or something monumental. It's nothing monumental! It's just deception! Just plain old-fashioned deception, that's all. Happens all the time. It's going on right now."

CECILIA: Mr Carter?

CARTER (*drinks and rants*): We almost pulled it off too. If it hadn't been for Simms, we woulda pulled it off. Simms could've closed one eye and no one would've been the wiser. We even offered him a piece of the action but he wouldn't take it.

CECILIA: Simms?

CARTER: Vinnie took the pictures, see. I had nothing to do with it. Vinnie set the whole thing up. Him and—this chippie he hired. It was him who rented the motel room. I told him it was going to backfire on him. Sooner or later. I told him that. Way back when he first got the idea.

CECILIA: Do you want me to call your wife for you?

CARTER: My wife?

CECILIA: Maybe you could talk to her.

CARTER: My wife?

*Pause.*

CECILIA: Yes. Don't you want to go back home, Mr Carter?

*Pause.* CARTER *is good and drunk by now, disoriented. He looks around the room, then stares at the window. He crosses to one of the windows and stares out.*

CECILIA: Is something wrong?

CARTER *opens the window, staring out.*

CECILIA: Mr Carter, you're starting to scare me. I'd be more than willing to call somebody for you. Is there anybody you would like to talk to?

CARTER (*staring out open window*): There's still a smell about the place. You know? Alfalfa. Dirt. A distant, vague smell of cut alfalfa. I noticed that when we were walking from the car. Did you notice that?

CECILIA: No. I'm not sure what alfalfa smells like.

CARTER (*stays at window*): Amazing. Alfalfa. Smells just like the earth. Me and Vinnie used to buck three wire bales right down the road there where the thrifty is. Right past there. Used to watch a horse named "Swaps" trot down the fence line with his neck bowed and his tail cocked high. You remember Swaps?

CECILIA: No.

CARTER: Never heard of Swaps? One tough racehorse. In his day.

CECILIA: Are you all right?

CARTER (*still at window*): You're on my side, aren't you Cecilia? When we get right down to it? You're not going to—betray me? Even though you might've kissed him. That's—forgivable. That's understandable. But you're not—deceiving me now, are you? You're not hiding something?

CECILIA: I'm from Missouri, Mr Carter. There's nowhere to hide in Missouri.

CARTER: I could trust you—I mean if I asked you to do something for me, you wouldn't double-cross me? You wouldn't go to Vinnie—You're not like the rest of them are you?

CECILIA: I'm not going to do anything illegal, if that's what you mean.

CARTER: No. None of us are. Nothing like that. I'd never ask you to break the law. I'm not a criminal.

CECILIA: I think you should try to get some sleep and think things over. Maybe in the morning—

CARTER *breaks away from window, back toward the bed and begins to wander again, drinking.*

CARTER: It's too late for that! It's too late for sleeping and waking and sleeping and waking. I've been doing that all my life and it hasn't helped.

CECILIA: I don't really want to get involved. I mean, Vinnie and me were just friends—

CARTER: This is strictly on the up-and-up, Cecilia. Best way to be in this business. Gotta protect your reputation. People find out sooner or later anyway.

CECILIA: I don't know anything about business or—

CARTER: I could get you box seats at the Derby, Cecilia. Free access to the Clubhouse. The Paddock. Mint juleps. The Inner Circle. You could meet the Governor!

CECILIA: The Derby?

CARTER: Yes. First class all the way. Deluxe. Understand? Wined and dined.

CECILIA: The Kentucky Derby?

CARTER: That's the one. Churchill Downs.

CECILIA: I've got nothing to wear.

CARTER: I'll take care of that. Don't worry about that.

CECILIA: But, I've got a job here—

CARTER: This is the chance of a lifetime, Cecilia! It's like no other horse race in the world. Impressions are stamped on you for life. Branded. The Twin Spires. The icy eyes of Laffit Pincay. The hands of Eddie Arcaro. The rippling muscle of Seattle Slew. These are things that never leave you, Cecilia. Things beyond seduction. Beyond lust!

CECILIA: I don't know, I've never—

CARTER: "My Old Kentucky Home"? They sing that, you know. They all sing that. The masses. Even the ones who don't know the words. Even the ones from Illinois and Wisconsin. They all want to be part of it. They're all dying to belong to something old and rooted in American earth. They're swept up in the frenzy. Have you ever felt that, Cecilia? Have you ever felt like throwing yourself to the dogs?

CECILIA: I've dreamed about it.

CARTER: Yes. But the dream is nothing. Wait 'til you see it in the flesh and blood.

*Pause.*

CECILIA: What do you want me to do?

*CARTER goes to cellular phone and dials* SIMMS' *number. Lights come up dimly on* SIMMS *again.*

CARTER (*as he dials*): I want you to talk to this man. Tell him you're coming. Tell him you're bringing him something. He'll know what it is.

CECILIA: What man?

CARTER: Tell him you're working for me. My personal representative. He'll understand. Here—Tell him.

CARTER *hands her the phone, once he's dialed the number.* CECILIA *takes it and stands there, waiting for* SIMMS *to answer but he doesn't.* CARTER *crosses to* VINNIE's *bed, takes another drink and lies down on his back. Phone keeps ringing.* SIMMS *stares at it and goes back to his work.*

CARTER (*lying on bed*): You make a move like this, Cecilia. A radical move. Just one little move and everything shifts. Everything falls into place behind it. It carries its own momentum. It's a frightening thing but it pays off in the end. You'll see. It pays big dividends. It has a power all its own. Like a force of nature.

CECILIA *stands there waiting for* SIMMS *to answer phone but he never does. Lights fade slowly to black on both sides as phone keeps ringing in* SIMMS' *office.*

# Act Three

## SCENE ONE

*Day. Place-name card that reads—"LEXINGTON". Split-stage right. Living room of* CARTER's *Kentucky mansion, very simple set with the impression of wealth. A sofa, glass table and carpet.* VINNIE *is standing in the room with his box tucked under his arm, facing a young and very attractice nanny named* KELLY. *She is dressed in a dark skirt, white blouse, short black heels and her hair done up in a bun. Lights up.*

KELLY: Did you uh—have an appointment with Mrs Carter or anything?

VINNIE: Does she take appointments now?

KELLY: Well, I mean—was she expecting you?

VINNIE: No, I don't think she was.

KELLY: How did you get in, exactly?

VINNIE: Through the back door.

ROSIE'S VOICE (*off stage*): Who is it, Kelly? Is someone there?

KELLY (*to* ROSIE): It's—I don't—

ROSIE'S VOICE (*off*): Don't send them away! Kelly?

KELLY: Yes, mam?

ROSIE'S VOICE: Don't send them away, all right? I'm in the mood for company! I can feel it coming on me!

KELLY: He's—(*To* VINNIE.) What's your name?

VINNIE: Webb. Vincent T. Webb.

KELLY (*to* ROSIE): It's a Mr Vincent T. Webb!

ROSIE'S VOICE: Vincent T. Webb?

KELLY: That's what he says!

ROSIE'S VOICE: Who in the world is that? Sounds like a lawyer! He's not a lawyer is he?

KELLY (*to* VINNIE): Are you a lawyer?

VINNIE: No. I'm a detective.

KELLY (*to* ROSIE): He's a detective!

ROSIE'S VOICE: A what!

KELLY (*to* ROSIE): A detective!

ROSIE'S VOICE: A detective?

KELLY: That's what he says.

ROSIE'S VOICE: Is something wrong? Has something happened?

KELLY (*to* VINNIE): Has something happened?

VINNIE: No. Nothing's happened.

KELLY: Nothing's happened!

ROSIE'S VOICE (*off*): I can't take any excitement, Kelly! My pills haven't kicked in!

KELLY (*to* VINNIE): She doesn't know you. I think you should just—

VINNIE: She knows me.

ROSIE'S VOICE: Has something happened to Carter! Is that it?

KELLY (*to* VINNIE): She says she doesn't know you.

ROSIE'S VOICE: Kelly!

KELLY: Mam?

ROSIE'S VOICE: Has something happened to Carter! Where's he from anyway? This detective.

KELLY (*to* VINNIE): Where are you from?

VINNIE: California.

KELLY (*to* ROSIE): California!

VINNIE (*to* KELLY): Cucamonga, California.

KELLY (*to* ROSIE): Cucamonga, California!

ROSIE'S VOICE: Cucamonga?

KELLY (*to* ROSIE): That's what he says!

ROSIE'S VOICE: Nobody's from Cucamonga! That's where Carter's from!

KELLY (*to* VINNIE): She says her husband's from there but nobody else is.

VINNIE: I *am* her husband.

   *Pause.* KELLY *stares at him.*

KELLY (*to* VINNIE): You'd better leave.

ROSIE'S VOICE (*off*): Don't let him leave, Kelly!

ROSIE *enters upstage, slightly hung over and rumpled, pulling the sash of her robe together, pulling a slipper on. She spots* VINNIE *and smiles.*

ROSIE (*to* VINNIE): Oh—I'm sorry. So *you're* the detective. I uh—slept in. I heard the taxi in the driveway. It was in my dream in fact. I love taxis. I don't know why. They remind me of town, I guess. So colorful. All that—local advertising. We get so—disconnected sometimes—out here. Don't we, Kelly?

KELLY: Yes, mam. Um—this gentleman came in through the back door.

ROSIE: I know. Isn't that something. A Backdoor Man! We have such a disregard for crime out here. We leave doors open. Keys in the car. It's disgusting. It's a wonder we're not all raped and murdered.

KELLY: He says he knows you.

ROSIE: Oh. He does? (*To* VINNIE.) I'm sorry. Mr—Webb, was it?

VINNIE: Yes.

*They shake hands.* VINNIE *is reluctant to let her hand go.*

ROSIE: From—Cucamonga?

VINNIE: That's right.

ROSIE: That's amazing. My husband's from Cucamonga. Originally. In the beginning.

VINNIE: Yes. I know.

ROSIE: This isn't *about* my husband, is it?

VINNIE: No.

ROSIE: He hasn't done something?

VINNIE: Not that I know of.

ROSIE: That's a relief. You never know these days. Even the most intimate relationships are full of surprises. I'm from Glendora, myself. You know Glendora?

VINNIE: Yes. I walk there every day.

ROSIE: You do?

VINNIE: When I'm there.

ROSIE: Oh, that makes me so homesick! You have no idea. Just the sound of it—"Glendora". Like a Spanish woman's hair or something! Grapefruit trees! Orange blossoms on the wind! The snow-capped San Gabriels! I suppose it's changed though. Over the years.

VINNIE: Yes. It has.

ROSIE: Lost its splendor.

VINNIE: Yes.

ROSIE: Oh, would you—Kelly, did you offer Mr Webb a drink?

KELLY: No, mam. I was—

ROSIE (*to* VINNIE): What would you like? Coffee? Coca-Cola? Iced tea?

VINNIE: Bourbon please.

ROSIE: Ah, good choice. I like an early jump-start myself. What kind?

VINNIE: Black Bush.

ROSIE: I'm not sure we have that particular one in stock, do we Kelly?

KELLY: Mam—

ROSIE: What is it, Kelly?

KELLY: This man says—he knows you.

ROSIE: Yes, I know that. You already told me that. We're repeating ourselves, aren't we, Kelly?

KELLY: He says he—

ROSIE: Would you please go see if we have any of that—(*To* VINNIE.) What was the name, Mr Webb?

VINNIE: Black Bush. Irish.

ROSIE: That's it. "Black Bush". Those Irish have a way with words, don't they? Go see if we have that, Kelly.

KELLY: Mam. He says he's your husband.

ROSIE: Go find the Black Bush, Kelly! Do it, now!

*Pause.* KELLY *exits.* ROSIE *watches her.* ROSIE *turns to* VINNIE. *They stare at each other. Pause.*

ROSIE: Would you like me to take your coat and uh—your package?

VINNIE: No thanks.

ROSIE: If you're wearing a sidearm under there it doesn't matter. We've seen that before around here. Kelly's seen it. It's old hat.

VINNIE: I'm not.

ROSIE: So, you haven't come to do me in then? Splatter my brains all over the carpet in a fit of jealous rage? (*Pause.*) You're a long way from home, Vinnie.

VINNIE: Yeah. I am.

ROSIE: Carter just went out to see you. Did you know that? That's what he said he was up to anyway. You didn't somehow miss him did you? "Ships in the night"?

VINNIE: No. I saw him.

ROSIE: Oh, good. Did you work things out? I know it's been a long and bitter negotiation.

VINNIE: He said you two were on the outs.

ROSIE: Who?

VINNIE: You and him.

ROSIE (*laughs*): Is that what he said? Just like that? "On the outs"! Those were *his* words?

*Pause.*

VINNIE: Is it okay if I—sit down?

ROSIE: Help yourself! *Mi casa es su casa*, Vinnie. You know that. Just like the old days. Nothing's changed.

VINNIE *sits on edge of sofa, clutching shoebox under his arm.*

ROSIE: So, what've you got, a bomb in the box or something? Gonna blow us all to Kingdom Come?

VINNIE: I'm not going to hurt you.

ROSIE: You're not still harboring something, are you Vinnie? That's not healthy. That's the kind of thing that leads to cancer and insanity.

VINNIE: I just wanted to see you.

ROSIE: Well, here I am! Still in the bloom of things. I never would've recognized *you* though, Vinnie. You've let yourself go. I was watching you from the window and I was asking myself, "Now who is this? Who in the world could this be, arriving by taxi, with a package under his arm?" It's not roses, is it Vinnie? Roses for Rosie?

VINNIE: No.

ROSIE: I didn't think so. Too short for roses. Too compact. Unless you've cut the stems off. Out of spite or something. Wouldn't that be a shame.

VINNIE: So, how did you know?

ROSIE: What.

VINNIE: How did you recognize me?

ROSIE: Oh. The voice. Something in the voice rang a bell. A kind of apologetic menace. I don't know how else to describe it.

VINNIE: I'm not going to hurt you.

ROSIE: I'd feel a lot more reassured if you didn't keep repeating that.

VINNIE: I just want you to know. I didn't come here for that.

ROSIE: Good. That's good news. Now we don't have to talk about it anymore, do we? (*Pause.*) So you met up with Carter then? How did that go?

VINNIE: All right.

ROSIE: He said you were in some kind of an emergency again. He left here in a big rush.

VINNIE: I am.

ROSIE: Still?

VINNIE: Yes. I'm at the end of my rope. I may not look like it but I am.

ROSIE: Well, actually, you *are* looking a little rough around the edges, Vinnie. I didn't want to say anything—

VINNIE: I got arrested.

ROSIE: Oh. That's too bad. When was that?

VINNIE: A while back. Couple weeks ago.

ROSIE: Well, I'm sorry to hear that, Vinnie. What was it this time?

VINNIE: Assault with a deadly weapon. Attempted manslaughter.

ROSIE: You've escalated.

VINNIE: It won't stick. Just—hysterical reaction, is all it was.

ROSIE: It wasn't Carter, was it?

VINNIE: What.

ROSIE: Did you assault Carter?

VINNIE: No. He's safe.

ROSIE: Where is he?

VINNIE: Out there. My place.

ROSIE: How come he's out there and you're here? What's going on, Vinnie?

VINNIE: He's—He took up with a woman out there.

*Pause.* ROSIE *stares at him.* KELLY *re-enters with a tray and drinks. Pause, as she sets the drinks down on glass table then turns to go.* ROSIE *stops her.*

ROSIE: Kelly?

KELLY (*stops*): Yes, mam?

ROSIE: What time are you picking up the kids today?

KELLY: Three o'clock. The usual time.

ROSIE: Doesn't Simon have band practice?

KELLY: No, not today. That's Thursdays.

ROSIE: Oh. Right. Well, look Kelly, why don't you take them to have ice cream and then go to Toys 'R' Us or something. All right? Just find something to do with them for a little while.

KELLY (*looks at* VINNIE): Okay.

ROSIE: I need to talk with Mr Webb here.

KELLY: All right.

> KELLY *starts to go, then stops. She eyes* VINNIE *then turns to* ROSIE.

KELLY (*to* ROSIE): Is everything—Are you sure you'll be all right, Mrs Carter?

ROSIE: I'm fine, Kelly. Just go get the kids now. Do as you're told.

> KELLY *eyes* VINNIE *again, then exits. Pause as* ROSIE *and* VINNIE *sip their drinks.*

ROSIE: So—he's run off with a woman. Not that I'm shocked or anything. He's been carrying on behind my back since day one.

VINNIE: When *was* that?

ROSIE: What?

VINNIE: "Day One".

ROSIE: We're not going to drag that back up out of the dirt, are we Vinnie? Things happened. One thing led to another. I don't know. It was a long time ago.

VINNIE: But now it's over, right?

ROSIE: What.

VINNIE: You and him?

ROSIE: Apparently so! What're you trying to tell me? He's shacked up with a woman at *your* place and you've come all the way out here to give me the good news?

VINNIE: He met this girl—

ROSIE: A girl! A girl! It's always a girl. Never a woman.

VINNIE: He met this girl in a bar out there.

ROSIE: What a surprise!

VINNIE: I guess she got infatuated with him.

ROSIE: Oh, *she* got infatuated with *him*!

VINNIE: I guess.

ROSIE: And you, very generously, donated your bed to the cause!

VINNIE: No—

ROSIE: And now you've gone out of your way, as a friend, to make sure I understand all the sordid details!

VINNIE (*sudden burst*): HE STOLE MY BUICK, ROSIE! HE STOLE MY BUICK AND HE STOLE MY WIFE!

*Pause.* ROSIE *stares at him.*

ROSIE: You know, for a long time I kept dreading this confrontation. I had little nightmares about it. But now that it's here, it seems dull actually. Stupid.

VINNIE: You could've left me a note or something.

ROSIE: A note!

VINNIE: Something.

ROSIE: Oh you mean like: "Gone to the 7–11 to get a six-pack. Be right back"?

VINNIE: Something. Not just—disappeared.

ROSIE: We were *all* checking out of there, Vinnie! *All* of us. That was the plan. Remember?

VINNIE: Yeah. I remember.

ROSIE: No contact. No trace of any connection between us.

VINNIE: That was the plan.

ROSIE: It's a little late for regrets.

VINNIE: I just thought maybe you'd—

ROSIE: What?

*Pause.*

VINNIE: Come back.

ROSIE: To what? Life on the backstretch? Fifteen-hundred-dollar claimers? I could've set up house in the back of a horse trailer, maybe?

VINNIE: We had fun. We had some fun.

ROSIE: Fun!

VINNIE: Read the Form 'til two in the morning sometimes. Picking long-shots. Clocking works.

ROSIE: Fun.

VINNIE: Slept in the truck bed. Listened to the tin roof flap on the shedrow.

ROSIE: Fun, fun, fun!

VINNIE: You could've called me or something.

ROSIE: What about *you*? Where have you been all this time?

VINNIE: I had no idea where you went.

ROSIE: Come on. You knew where the checks were coming from. You knew the phone number well enough.

VINNIE: I didn't want to—interrupt your life.

ROSIE: Get outa here.

VINNIE: I thought you and Carter were—

ROSIE: What.

VINNIE: Getting along. I mean—

ROSIE: *You're* the one who disappeared, Vinnie. *You're* the one who vanished.

VINNIE: I'm here, now.

ROSIE: Well, isn't that great! Isn't that dandy! Fifteen years later you sneak through my back door with a dumb box and a hang-dog look on your face.

VINNIE: I wasn't sneaking.

ROSIE: What'd you come here for?

*Pause.*

VINNIE: I thought maybe I could set things straight.

ROSIE: What *things*?

VINNIE: I uh—found Simms. I went and talked to him.

ROSIE: Who?

VINNIE: Simms. "Ames", as he's called now.

ROSIE: I don't know who you're talking about.

VINNIE: He seems to have reconciled something with himself. No malice. He lives in his own little world. Studies bloodlines and stays out of trouble.

ROSIE: What're we talking about here?

VINNIE: He's the kind of man who was able to rebound from terrible shock and pull himself back together. He had no interest whatsoever in what I had to offer.

ROSIE: And what was that?

VINNIE: These.

*VINNIE holds out the shoebox to her. She doesn't take it from him.*

ROSIE: What's in there? Dead puppies?

VINNIE: Take it.

*ROSIE slowly takes the box and puts her hand on the lid but doesn't open it.*

ROSIE: Is a snake going to jump out at me or something? A tiny nightmare?

VINNIE: Open it.

*Pause.*

ROSIE: I just love surprises.

*She slowly lifts the lid and stares at the contents, then suddenly drops the box, spilling photos, letters etc. and starts yelling for the nanny. She moves nervously around the room.*

ROSIE (*yelling to off stage*): KELLY! KELLY, ARE YOU STILL THERE! KELLY GET BACK HERE! KELLY!!

*VINNIE drops to his hands and knees and starts quickly collecting the fallen articles and putting them back in the box.*

VINNIE (*on hands and knees collecting photos*): Now don't get excited. I was going to *give* them to you. I was going to give them all to you. Simms doesn't want them so I was going to just hand them over to you.

ROSIE: Who is Simms! I don't know this man! I have never heard of this man! (*To off-stage.*) KELLY!

VINNIE: Not on a long–term basis maybe.

ROSIE: Not on any kinda basis! Now get outa here!

VINNIE: Just a fling. Just a one–night stand in a Motel 6 on the edge of Azusa!

*Long pause.*

ROSIE: Now who is going to believe that? Who in the world is going to believe something like that? After all this time.

VINNIE: It's all right here. Pictures don't lie.

ROSIE: Take a look. Take a long hard look at that face. (*Referring to photo.*) Does that even remotely resemble someone we know?

VINNIE (*looking at photo*): It was a long time ago.

ROSIE: Pick all this shit up and get outa here. Now!

VINNIE *slowly rises with shoebox and contents.*

VINNIE: I was going to give it all back to you. You can burn it if you want to. I was gonna trade you straight across.

ROSIE: Trade me? Trade me for what?

VINNIE: I had this idea in my head. I had it all cooked up. I was gonna get another Buick. Just like the one I had. You remember that Buick?

ROSIE: No.

VINNIE: You remember me driving with one hand on the wheel and the other one on your knee?

ROSIE: No, I don't.

VINNIE: I was thinking maybe we could still run off together.

ROSIE: Run off? I'm a married woman, Vinnie! Where're we gonna run off to now?

VINNIE: I don't know. Mexico maybe.

ROSIE: Oh Jesus, Vinnie. Give it up! Everything has already happened! It's already taken place. This is it. There's no "running off" anymore. It's a done deal. You're in your little hell and I'm in mine.

VINNIE: It's not done!

*VINNIE suddenly grabs her and pulls her violently to him. He tries to kiss her but she pushes him away. They stand apart. Pause.*

ROSIE (*low, menacing*): You touch me—You so much as touch me again and I'll have you killed. This is *my* house. I'm the wife of someone. Someone of tremendous power and influence. He could have you done in from a distance and you wouldn't even know what hit you. I don't care who he's sleeping with—all it would take is a call from me. One little phone call and you'd be history, Vincent T. Webb. He'd do anything for me, Vinnie. Anything at all. And do you know why that is? Do you have any kind of clue, Vinnie? Because he *owes* me. He's deeply in debt to me. All from that one little brainstorm of mine, way back then. That one little night on the edge of Azusa.

VINNIE: Oh, so now you're suddenly gonna take all the credit.

ROSIE: Yeah, sure. Why not? It was a brilliant little notion. It paid off in spades too, didn't it? I probably shoulda just gone professional.

VINNIE: I took the pictures!

ROSIE: You certainly did. But *I* turned the trick. It was me who caused the heads to roll and don't you ever forget it.

VINNIE: I won't. I won't ever forget it.

*Pause.*

ROSIE: Did you actually think—You didn't actually think that—

VINNIE: What?

ROSIE: That's unbelievable—after all this time. Mexico?

VINNIE: It was just an idea.

ROSIE: Mexico?

VINNIE *hands her the shoebox as the lights fade.*

## SCENE TWO

*Midway, Ky. Split-stage left.* SIMMS' *office again.* SIMMS *habitually hovering over his desk, pouring through papers and drinking. He's already had several drinks and is much more well-oiled than the first time he was seen.* CECILIA *stands nervously across the desk from him, dressed in her crisp new "Derby" outfit—brightly flowered dress, straw hat, white high heels, white gloves and a large purse stuffed with cash. Pause, as she watches* SIMMS *at work, mumbling, scratching notes with his pen and seemingly oblivious to her presence.*

CECILIA: I can come back, if you like. I didn't realize you were going to be so busy.

SIMMS (*staying with his work, not looking up at her*): No, no, no. Why come back when you're already here. Don't you worry. Everything's an interruption when you're working on bloodlines. It's an endless chain. Never get to the bottom of it. Just when you think you've discovered the key to the most mysterious breeding nick in the history of racing, the glaring truth of it all reaches up and slaps you right in the face.

CECILIA: I see.

SIMMS: No you don't.

CECILIA: Well, I was just wondering if—

SIMMS (*not looking up at her*): The glaring truth is that every single solitary thoroughbred horse in the world—living or dead—and all those foals yet to be born are, in one way or another, related by blood. From the glue factory to the winner's circle—each and every one of them carries some common factor, miniscule as it may be. So it's somewhat futile, don't you think, to try and factor out this elusive element of speed in the midst of such a vast genetic ocean. Even worse folly to attempt to identify what gives a thoroughbred heart.

CECILIA: Heart?

SIMMS: Yes. The guts to run. The guts to win. Courage—to put it plain.

CECILIA: That's amazing.

SIMMS: It is.

CECILIA: I never realized it was so—complex.

SIMMS (*finally looks up at her*): It's not. It's our vain efforts that make it that way.

SIMMS *stares at her. Pause.*

CECILIA: I—

*Pause.* SIMMS *keeps staring.*

CECILIA: I—don't know exactly how to put this but—

SIMMS: You're stunning.

CECILIA: What?

SIMMS: You're absolutely stunning.

CECILIA (*blushing*): Well, thank you. That's very kind.

SIMMS: Where did you come from?

CECILIA: I'm—You know—

SIMMS: Have you been standing there long? I'm very sorry. I tend to get absorbed. I didn't mean to be rude.

CECILIA: No, no—That's quite all right. It's fascinating stuff. I don't know anything about horses, myself.

SIMMS: Do you uh—Would you like a drink or—

CECILIA: No, thank you. I don't drink.

SIMMS *gets up and stumbles slightly, heading for his liquor cabinet.*

SIMMS: Oh. Well—You won't mind if I—

*He fixes himself a fresh bourbon on ice.*

CECILIA: No, please. Go right ahead.

SIMMS: Helps to keep the wheels churning. A little lubrication.

CECILIA: Yes.

SIMMS: You uh—You're in the horse business, I take it?

CECILIA: No, I'm not. I'm—an associate of Mr Carter's. I thought he talked to you about me. He was going to call and—

SIMMS: An associate?

CECILIA: Yes. We tried to call you but your phone was off the hook or something and he said he was going to let you know I was coming.

SIMMS: I despise the phone. Don't you?

CECILIA: Well—

SIMMS: The cloning of the phone. Another disease, don't you think?

CECILIA: I don't really—

SIMMS: Another desperate measure.

CECILIA: Didn't Mr Carter tell you I was coming?

SIMMS: Carter? Carter. That's funny. Another acquaintance of his popped in just the other morning.

CECILIA: Vinnie?

SIMMS: Oh, you know him then? Very disturbed individual, I thought. Very agitated. Lying through his teeth.

CECILIA: He's high strung.

SIMMS: Is that what it is?

CECILIA: He's had a string of bad luck.

SIMMS: Oh—well, that'll do it all right.

*Pause.* SIMMS *stares at her again.* CECILIA *squirms, nervously.*

SIMMS: You're absolutely gorgeous. I can't get over it.

CECILIA: Well, thank you very much.

SIMMS: You don't understand what kind of a storm you've begun to arouse inside me. I mean—I must be visibly shaking. Am I shaking? Can you see me shaking?

CECILIA: No, I—

SIMMS: You're just being polite.

CECILIA: I really, just want to—

SIMMS: If you knew—if you had the slightest clue as to the pounding that's going on in my cardiovascular system, you'd be able to manipulate me to your heart's content.

CECILIA: I don't—

SIMMS: That must've been Carter's intention, right?

CECILIA: No! He just—

SIMMS: You'd be able to have me groveling at your feet. Is that what he wants?

CECILIA: No!

SIMMS: Would you like to see me grovel?

*SIMMS goes down on one knee, holding his drink.*

CECILIA: No, please! Please don't do that!

SIMMS: Beg? Lick your boots? Kiss the ground you walk on?

*SIMMS crawls toward her with his tongue lapping out. CECILIA backs up fast.*

CECILIA (*backing up*): DON'T DO THAT! STAY AWAY!

*SIMMS stops, then slowly rises to his feet and returns to his desk with his drink.*

SIMMS: I'm sorry. I didn't mean to alarm you. It's been a long day.

CECILIA: I'm very flattered that you think I'm—attractive. But it's got nothing to do with why I came.

SIMMS (*suddenly curious*): This isn't Sunday, is it?

*He turns and looks out the window, then looks back at CECILIA.*

CECILIA: Sunday? No, I don't—I don't think so. Why?

SIMMS: Your outfit smacks of Sunday. Church. Spanking clean. Very Protestant.

CECILIA: Oh. It's my new Derby dress.

SIMMS: Derby?

CECILIA: Yes. My Kentucky Derby dress. I—I just bought it.

SIMMS: This is October, isn't it? Aren't we in October now?

CECILIA: We are?

SIMMS: Yes. I'm sure of it. (*Turns to window again.*) Look—the trees are turning gold. There's a chill in the air. Jack o' lanterns in every window. They wouldn't do that if it wasn't October.

CECILIA: Who?

SIMMS: Citizens. Those who play the game.

CECILIA: Oh, that's right.

SIMMS: The Derby's in May. First Saturday in May, to be exact.

CECILIA: I know but—

SIMMS: You're early. Or late, as the case may be.

CECILIA: I know. I was just trying it out.

SIMMS: Trying it out on *me*?

CECILIA: Mr Carter bought it for me and I thought I'd—

SIMMS: Carter.

CECILIA: It was his money.

SIMMS: He's a generous man.

CECILIA: He is.

*Pause.* SIMMS *stares at her.*

SIMMS: Have a seat, Miss—

CECILIA: Pontz. Cecilia Pontz. From Missouri.

CECILIA *remains tensely standing.* SIMMS *sits in his chair.*

SIMMS: A prairie flower!

CECILIA: I don't want to take up a lot of your time, Mr Ames.

SIMMS: Neither did the other man. But he did.

CECILIA: Excuse me?

SIMMS: Webb. He consumed a good half hour trying to convince me that vengeance was the best row to hoe. How do you feel about it, Miss Ponds? An eye for an eye?

CECILIA: Pontz. With a "z".

SIMMS: Pontz, with a "z". How do you feel about it?

CECILIA: What?

SIMMS: Vengeance.

CECILIA: I don't—I haven't thought about it much.

SIMMS: No. And why should you? You're in the Spring of life.

CARTER: Well, thank you.

SIMMS: Not your fault. It's genetics. All in the genes. We've got nothing to do with it. It was all decided generations ago. Faceless ancestors. The curvature of your hips. You can't possibily take credit for that now, can you?

CECILIA: Um—

SIMMS: The turn of your lips. Who first sculpted that in your far-away past?

CECILIA: I really—

SIMMS: Please, have a seat. You're looking flustered.

CECILIA: Oh. Thank you. Thank you very much.

*She sits nervously in chair across from desk, clutching her bag.* SIMMS *reaches across desk to relieve her of the bag.*

SIMMS (*reaching*): Would you like me to take your bag?

CECILIA: No!

*She whips the bag away from him and protects it.*

CECILIA: No, thank you. I've got some private things in there.

SIMMS (*standing, stretched across desk*): Underpants?

CECILIA: Excuse me?

SIMMS (*sitting back in his chair*): Never mind. Sure you won't have a little tipple? Might loosen you up some.

CECILIA: No, I'm fine.

SIMMS: You certainly are, Miss Pontz. You certainly are that.

CECILIA: Um—Mr Webb—the other man—The man who paid you a visit—

SIMMS: The idiot. Yes?

CECILIA: Did he—Did he sell you something?

SIMMS: He sold me a bill of goods, if that's what you mean.

CECILIA: No, I mean—

SIMMS: Yes. That's what you're here for. Isn't it?

CECILIA: Well—

SIMMS: How did you get mixed up with those two knot-heads, Miss Ponds? A bright-eyed gal from Missouri.

CECILIA: Well, Mr Carter's an old friend of Vinnie's and I'd known Vinnie from before.

SIMMS: I see.

CECILIA: They've known each other since childhood.

SIMMS: Thick as flies.

CECILIA: But—they've gone separate ways. Something happened, I guess. Some—schism.

SIMMS: Separate ways?

CECILIA: Yes. They're like opposites now.

SIMMS: The right and left hand.

CECILIA: Excuse me?

SIMMS: Nothing. Your innocence is almost as shocking as your beauty.

CECILIA: I've—I'm sorry—I've never heard anyone talk like that. I just don't know what to say. I'm—

SIMMS: Speechless.

CECILIA: I'm trying to present something to you but you're making it very, very difficult! I came as a messenger from Mr Carter. He wants you to know—He wants to give you an alternative to the deal you've struck with Mr Webb. A better deal.

SIMMS: Have you laid down with him, Miss Ponds?

CECILIA: What!

SIMMS: Your Mr Carter—Have you done the down and dirty deed with him? Spread your magnificent thighs?

CECILIA *stands abruptly, drops her bag and fumbles to retrieve it.*

CECILIA: No! Of course not. I've only recently met him. Now listen, you have no right to—

SIMMS: You're not a high-paid chippie then? A Class Act? Something found in the Yellow Pages under "Executive Escorts"?

CECILIA: I don't need to be insulted, Mr Ames!

SIMMS: Nobody does, but you evidently, haven't got the full picture, Miss Cecilia from Missouri. Either that or you're dumber than a fence post.

CECILIA: Mr Carter simply wanted me to ask if you'd consider selling the negatives—the material—for a slightly higher price than you paid for them. That's all. Now I'd appreciate it if you were as straightforward with me as I'm attempting to be with you. He's offering a good deal of money. I've got it right here. (*She pats her bag.*) Cash. It's all present and accounted for.

SIMMS (*smiling*): Cash.

CECILIA: That's right. You *did* call him, didn't you? You *did* make some kind of an—overture. I was right there when you called.

SIMMS: You took a hot shower and shampoo; put on your crisp "Derby" dress; filled your purse with a "good deal of cash" and flew all the way out here, just to see me?

CECILIA: Yes. That's exactly right.

SIMMS: That's so sweet. It makes my skin tingle to think of you doing all that just for me.

CECILIA: I don't think you understand.

SIMMS: You're making me a proposition.

CECILIA: Yes, but it's got nothing to do with—

SIMMS: How 'bout Vinnie? Mr Vinnie. Have you laid down with him?

CECILIA: Do you want to sell the negatives or not, Mr Ames! Yes or no!

SIMMS (*chuckles*): The "negatives", the "negatives". What are these mysterious negatives?

CECILIA: You bought them, didn't you! You know very well what they are.

SIMMS: I heard they were of a libidinous nature. Is that true?

CECILIA: I don't know what that means.

SIMMS: "Off-color". "Lewd". "Racy". "Ruttish".

CECILIA: Yes. They are.

SIMMS: How "ruttish", Miss Cecilia?

CECILIA: Look—I don't have to explain to you—

SIMMS: Did they arouse your prurient interest? Did you get excited when you first saw them? You *have* seen them, haven't you?

CECILIA: Yes! I've seen them.

SIMMS: You've examined them closely?

CECILIA: I've seen them!

SIMMS: Well?

CECILIA: I can only say that anyone who would allow themselves to be photographed in those positions—

SIMMS: "Allowed"? Let me just explain something to you, Miss Pontz with a "z", that these two bandits, Webb and Carter, may have neglected to tell you—

CECILIA *begins to move around very nervously, clutching at her chest and having difficulty breathing. Like a sudden asthma attack.*

CECILIA: Would you—Would you mind opening up a window? I'm suddenly—short of breath. I feel like I'm suffocating or something.

SIMMS: Of course. (*Goes to window and opens it.*) Sure you wouldn't like to have a drink? It helps sometimes in moments like this.

CECILIA: No, I—I don't know what it is. My chest—It'll pass.

SIMMS: Hot flashes?

CECILIA: No!

SIMMS: Do you live alone, Miss Pontz?

CECILIA: WOULD YOU BE INTERESTED IN SELLING THE NEGATIVES, MR SIMMS! Or not. Please— just—I can't take much more of this. I'm not cut out for this. I work in the Safeway!

SIMMS: "Simms"? Is that what you called me?

CECILIA: I mean—Ames. Mr Ames. You know who you are! I've seen you! I've seen who you are! Don't pretend with me.

SIMMS (*moving back to desk*): You're a little mixed up, aren't you, Cecilia? A little bit scrambled.

CECILIA: I shouldn't have come here at all. I didn't want to be doing this. I've never done anything like this before in my life!

SIMMS: But your pals talked you into it?

CECILIA: They're not my "pals"! I hardly even know them.

SIMMS: They're snakes, Cecilia. That's exactly what they are. They crawl on their bellies.

*Pause.*

CECILIA: I just—All I really wanted to do was go to the Kentucky Derby. That's all. And Mr Carter offered me free tickets. The Clubhouse. I don't know.

SIMMS: The Derby.

CECILIA: Yes. It was foolish to get suckered in by something like that but—I love the Derby. I've always—I—I remember being in London. It rained all the time. Always raining. And I—I would stay in and watch the races. I remember watching that big red horse—That magnificent red horse. What was his name? He was on the news. Everybody knew his name.

SIMMS: Secretariat.

CECILIA: Yes! That's the one. Secretariat. And he won by miles that day. Twenty lengths or something.

SIMMS: Thirty-one.

CECILIA: Yes. Thirty-one lengths. It was incredible. I've never seen an animal like that. As though he was flying.

SIMMS: He was.

CECILIA: He was like that winged horse they used to have on the gas stations, you know—That red, winged horse.

SIMMS: Pegasus.

CECILIA: Yes! Just like Pegasus. Ever since then I've dreamed of going to the Derby.

SIMMS: That wasn't the Derby you were watching. That was the Belmont.

CECILIA: Oh. It was?

SIMMS: Yes. It was. New York: 1973. He smashed the world record for a mile and a half. Demolished it.

CECILIA: He did? I don't know. I just remember him, flying. He was on the news.

SIMMS: There'll never be another one like him. Do you know what his heart weighed, Miss Pontz?

CECILIA: His heart? They weighed his heart? How horrible.

SIMMS: Twenty-two pounds.

CECILIA: They actually weighed his heart?

SIMMS: Twenty-two pounds. Do you know what the weight of an average thoroughbred's heart is? Just an average, run-of-the-mill, thoroughbred horse that can't pay his own feed bill?

CECILIA: I don't know a thing about horses.

SIMMS: Eight pounds.

CECILIA: I can't believe they weighed his heart. That means they—cut him open? Dug inside?

SIMMS: That's a difference of fourteen pounds.

CECILIA: How could they do that to such a wonderful animal? Cut his heart out.

SIMMS: Treachery, Miss Pontz. Pure and simple, treachery.

*Pause.*

CECILIA: Well—

SIMMS: Sure you won't have a drink?

CECILIA: I should be going. I don't know what ever made me think I could go through with something like this. I'm from the Mid-West.

SIMMS: Why don't you have a drink? Just a smidgeon.

*Pause.*

CECILIA: All right. That might be—

SIMMS: There ya go! Are you breathing easier now?

SIMMS *moves to liquor cabinet and fixes her a bourbon.*

CECILIA: What?

SIMMS: You said you were suffocating.

CECILIA: Oh—Yes—I don't know what happened. It just suddenly came over me. A panic of some kind. I've had it before but—not for a long time. A pressure on the chest.

SIMMS: And it suddenly returned?

CECILIA: I guess so. Has that ever happened to you? As though you've lost track of everything. I was standing there and all of a sudden, I didn't recognize myself at all. I had no idea what I was doing here. This dress—

SIMMS: You're so unbelievably beautiful, it makes my mouth dry.

CECILIA: Why do you—Why do you keep saying things like that? Are you trying to—

SIMMS (*crosses to her with drink*): Seduce you? No. I'm past that, Miss Pontz. Way past that. This dog can't hunt anymore but he still gets "birdie". Bourbon?

*Pause. He holds drink out to her. She takes it.*

CECILIA: Thank you.

SIMMS: My pleasure.

*Pause. She sips.*

CECILIA: How could you—have done something like that?

SIMMS: Like what?

CECILIA: Like what you did in those pictures. You don't seem like the kind of man—

SIMMS: Well, some of us get caught with our pants down and some don't. I was one of the lucky ones.

CECILIA: Lucky?

SIMMS: I got over it.

CECILIA: But you must have—suffered.

SIMMS: It's all in the past. Now it's their turn.

CECILIA: They—set you up, then?

SIMMS: Bingo!

CECILIA: The two of them? I can't believe it. I feel so foolish.

*He clicks glasses with hers and drinks.*

SIMMS: At least you got a new dress outa the deal.

*Pause.*

CECILIA: Well, I should get back. I should take this money back to him.

SIMMS: How much money *is* there, in your—purse, Miss Pontz?

CECILIA: What? Oh—I don't really know. I never counted it.

SIMMS: A great deal.

CECILIA: Yes. I suppose. I've never seen so much money in my whole life, in fact. Last night—last night I did a funny thing. I was in my motel room. I was alone in there and—I was naked. And—I don't know why, but I laid all the money out on the bed. All of it. I covered the whole bed with it. And I—laid down on top of it and— fell asleep. It was funny. I've never done anything like that before. When I woke up I thought I was laying on leaves. Wet leaves.

SIMMS: Well, we all do strange things in the face of sudden fortune.

CECILIA: I should really get going. Thanks for the drink.

*She moves to his desk and sets the glass of bourbon down on it, then turns to leave.*

SIMMS: Miss Pontz—

*She stops and turns to him.*

CECILIA: What?

SIMMS: I was just wondering—since you've got the new dress and everything—if maybe you'd consider going to the Derby with *me*?

CECILIA: The Derby?

SIMMS: Yes.

CECILIA: That's in May, isn't it?

SIMMS: Yes. It is.

CECILIA: But we're in October.

SIMMS: That's right.

CECILIA: There's all those months in between.

SIMMS: We could—There's all that cash.

*Pause.*

CECILIA: No, I couldn't do that. That's not right.

SIMMS: We could travel.

CECILIA: No. I've got to get back.

SIMMS: We could take a ship.

CECILIA (*smiles*): No. Thanks anyway.

*Pause.*

SIMMS: If you change your mind—I'll meet you at the Clubhouse Turn.

CECILIA: That's in May?

SIMMS: Yes. First Saturday.

*Lights dim. Cross-fade to Scene Three.*

## SCENE THREE

*Cucamonga. Split-stage right—*VINNIE's *room.* CARTER *is lying in* VINNIE's *bed in T-shirt, boxer shorts, socks on, wrapped up tightly in blankets with the shakes. His teeth are chattering and he rolls slightly from side to side. His clothes are tossed in a heap on the foot of the bed. His cellular phone is on the floor in the briefcase.* VINNIE *is slowly perusing the room, checking out the sink and the absence of his dirty laundry. Pause as* CARTER *softly moans and rocks himself in the blankets.*

VINNIE: Somebody, uh—did the laundry, I guess, huh? Dishes?

CARTER: Yeah.

VINNIE: You—hired somebody? I told you I didn't want that.

CARTER: No. Your girl. You know—Cecilia.

VINNIE: *She* did the laundry?

CARTER: Yeah.

VINNIE: She shouldn't of done that. Why'd you let her do that?

CARTER: She—wanted to.

VINNIE: So you brought her over here, I guess.

CARTER: Yeah. That was the plan. That's what you asked me to do. Remember?

VINNIE: We had a plan?

CARTER: You said you needed to talk to her! You were desperate.

VINNIE: That's right. I was. Desperate.

CARTER: What happened? Where were you?

VINNIE: I was—called away on business.

CARTER: Right.

*Pause.* VINNIE *moves over to him and stops.*

VINNIE: Why are you shaking, Carter? What's the deal? What is the problem here. Why are you in my bed?

CARTER: I'm—I don't know. At first I thought it was—the booze. You know—The—general shock to the system. I mean I'm not used to straight bourbon I guess, after all those years of nothing but cocktails.

VINNIE: You drank all my bourbon?

VINNIE *checks under bed, finds bourbon gone.*

CARTER: I'll get you another bottle.

VINNIE: Where? They don't carry Black Bush down at the 7–11, Carter. Where are you going to get me another bottle of Black Bush?

VINNIE *stands over* CARTER.

CARTER: Where did *you* get it?

VINNIE: I'll have to go a long way now. A long way out of my way.

CARTER: I'll find it for you. Don't worry.

VINNIE: I'll have to go on foot.

CARTER: I'll find it, all right! Don't worry about that!

*Pause.* VINNIE *moves around the space.*

VINNIE: You were messing with my stuff, too, weren't you?

CARTER: What stuff?

VINNIE: My boxes. They've been moved around. I can tell by the dust marks.

CARTER: No.

VINNIE: I can tell, Carter. (*Pause.*) Were you looking for something?

CARTER: No.

*Pause.*

VINNIE: So, where's Cecilia now? Where's she gone to?

CARTER: She—left. I don't know.

VINNIE: She came and left.

CARTER: Yeah.

VINNIE: She washed the dishes, did the laundry and left?

CARTER: Yeah.

VINNIE: What a gal.

CARTER: We waited for you. We waited for hours and then—

VINNIE: Drinking my bourbon.

CARTER: Well, she doesn't drink, you know—

VINNIE: Yes! I know that. I'm well aware of that!

CARTER: She wouldn't touch it.

VINNIE: Did you try to get her to?

CARTER: What?

VINNIE: Touch it?

CARTER: Look—

VINNIE: Get out of my bed, Carter.

CARTER: I'm—not sure I can.

VINNIE: Have you tried? Have you made a stab at it?

CARTER: My legs gave out.

> VINNIE *crosses to him. Stops at bed.*

VINNIE: What's going on with you?

CARTER: I don't know—I keep breaking out in cold sweats. My spine—

VINNIE: Your spine?

CARTER: My whole back gets frozen.

VINNIE: You want some uh—Alka-Seltzer Plus maybe? I've got some of that. Advil?

CARTER: No.

VINNIE: Tylenol? Extra-Strength.

CARTER: No.

VINNIE: Well, what, exactly, do you need, Carter? An ambulance?

CARTER: You went to Simms! Didn't you? You sold the stuff to Simms. Am I right? He called me, you know. Trying to deal behind your back. He told me the whole story.

*Pause.*

VINNIE: I am exhausted. Every part of me is wiped out. I need my bed. Do you understand that? I need my bed now! This is *my* bed!

CARTER: And then you went to see Rosie. Didn't you? I know you did. I know you, Vinnie.

*Pause.*

VINNIE: Are you going to get out of my bed or am I going to have to get ugly?

*Pause.*

CARTER: I'll give it a try.

VINNIE: Ata boy! What a trooper.

> CARTER *sits up slowly, shaking. He makes a great effort to swing his legs over the side and stand.* VINNIE *just watches him but makes no attempt to help.*

CARTER (*as he struggles*): What'd she say when she saw you! That must've been something, huh? Quite a little shock. Did she recognize you?

VINNIE: Yeah. She did.

CARTER: After all these years?

VINNIE: She knew, right off the bat.

CARTER: Just like old times, huh?

VINNIE: Nothing's changed.

CARTER: She's—still looking pretty good, isn't she? For a woman her age.

VINNIE: In the pink.

CARTER (*struggling to stand*): And she—She was glad to see you, I guess.

VINNIE: She was thrilled.

CARTER (*shaky, trying to remain standing*): Did she—throw her arms around you?

VINNIE: Yes. She did.

CARTER: Squeeze you?

VINNIE: She couldn't get enough of me.

CARTER (*still standing*): But you didn't—I mean, the kids were there. The nanny.

VINNIE: The kids were in school.

CARTER: But the nanny—Kelly.

VINNIE: She was there.

CARTER: So you didn't—I mean you just *hugged*, right? You and Rosie—You just—

CARTER *collapses back into the bed.* VINNIE *stands over him.*

VINNIE: Are you going to get out of my bed or not?

CARTER: I can't.

*Pause.* VINNIE *suddenly grabs* CARTER *by the ankles and jerks him off the bed, onto the floor.* CARTER *just lies there in a heap. Pause.* VINNIE *takes his coat off and lies down on the bed. He stretches and clasps his hands behind his head, stares at the ceiling. Pause.* CARTER *is shivering.*

CARTER (*from floor*): Could I—have a blanket?

VINNIE: No!

CARTER: I'm freezing.

VINNIE: You're pathetic.

CARTER: I don't know what it is—

VINNIE: You shouldn't fool with bourbon, Carter. It needs respect. You've got no respect.

CARTER: It's not that. It's not *just* that.

VINNIE: Oh. What is it then? Are you having a breakdown? A general crack-up? Is that it?

CARTER: I'm freezing.

*VINNIE snatches up one of the blankets and tosses it to CARTER. CARTER wraps himself up tightly in it and begins to roll slowly from side to side, lying on the floor.*

CARTER: Thanks.

*Pause. CARTER continues to rock slowly. VINNIE stares at the ceiling.*

VINNIE: How long do you expect these symptoms to continue?

CARTER: I don't know. It's never happened to me before. If I—should suddenly die, Vinnie—

VINNIE: You're not gonna die.

CARTER: I'm just saying—if I do.

VINNIE: You're not gonna suddenly die! You're not gonna get out of it that easy.

CARTER: No. I'm just saying—It happens all the time. Out of the blue. People—keel over with no prior indications. No symptoms whatsoever. It just—happens.

VINNIE: There's usually some hint of something. Some history.

CARTER: NOT IN MY CASE!!

*Pause. CARTER keeps rocking slowly, on the floor. VINNIE keeps staring at the ceiling.*

VINNIE: Could you stop that rolling around please. It's irritating. I'm trying to get some rest. I need rest now.

CARTER *stops rocking but keeps shaking. Pause.*

CARTER: So—What'd you and Rosie talk about?

VINNIE: The past.

CARTER: High school? The racetrack?

VINNIE: Just the past. In general.

CARTER: Did she—mention me at all?

VINNIE: No.

CARTER: Didn't she ask about me? I mean—she knew I was coming out here to see you and then you show up out *there.* Didn't she wonder about that?

VINNIE: I guess not.

*Pause.* CARTER *starts to rock back and forth again in the blanket.* VINNIE *stays on bed.*

CARTER: So—You must've made a killing off of Simms, huh? How much did he give you?

VINNIE: Bookoos.

CARTER: Well, it couldn't have been *that* much.

VINNIE: It was plenty.

CARTER: I know how much he makes a month so it couldn't have been all that much.

VINNIE: He cut me in on some shares. "Danzig". "Mr Prospector". Stuff like that. Big shares.

*Pause.*

CARTER: Do you think he's going to—

VINNIE: What?

CARTER: Get vindictive?

VINNIE: I wouldn't be at all surprised.

CARTER: You don't think he'll—go to the press or anything? Try to take it back to court?

VINNIE: I wouldn't be a bit surprised.

CARTER: He wouldn't go to the press. He'd never let those pictures out. They'd never print them anyway.

VINNIE: So, what're you worried about?

CARTER: I don't know. I just feel like—my number's up.

*Pause.* CARTER *keeps rocking slowly.*

VINNIE: When do you think you might *feel* like getting my bourbon?

CARTER: I can't walk.

VINNIE: Have you tried?

CARTER: I can hardly stand up.

VINNIE *sits up fast on bed.*

VINNIE: WILL YOU STOP THAT ROCKING BACK AND FORTH! STOP IT!

CARTER *stops.*

VINNIE (*from bed*): Now, sit up. Sit up, Carter!

CARTER *struggles to a sitting position. Very shaky.*

VINNIE: Now stand.

CARTER *struggles, but can't stand.* VINNIE *lunges off the bed, grabs* CARTER *by the chest and yanks him up to his feet, ripping the blanket away.*

VINNIE (*as he grabs* CARTER): STAND UP!

VINNIE *slaps him hard across the face. Just once. He holds him there.*

VINNIE: Now what in the hell's going on with you? I want you to put your clothes on. Pull yourself together and go out and buy me a bottle of bourbon! You *owe* me a bottle of bourbon.

CARTER: Where?

VINNIE: Just get dressed! I'll tell you *where* when you get your clothes back on.

CARTER *stumbles towards his clothes and starts trying to put them on but can't manage it.*

VINNIE: I have never seen anybody make such a big deal out of a hangover.

CARTER: It's not just that.

VINNIE: That's all it is! Amateur drinking! That's all it is!

CARTER: I'm completely cut off, Vinnie! I'm dying.

*Pause.*

VINNIE: What the fuck are you talking about? You weren't *dying* a couple a' days ago. You were full of yourself. You were strutting around here like a Banty rooster.

CARTER: I'm dying now.

VINNIE: Have you caught something? Have you found out that you *have* something?

CARTER: That would be easy, wouldn't it?

VINNIE: Easy?

CARTER: That would be understandable.

VINNIE: Do you want me to take you to the Emergency Room?

CARTER: You don't drive. Remember?

VINNIE: You can drive yourself. I'll go along with you. I'll ride shotgun.

CARTER: No.

VINNIE: No, what?

CARTER: I'm not going to the Emergency Room! It's past that.

VINNIE: You're giving up the ghost?

CARTER (*still struggling to dress*): I'm dying.

VINNIE: Stop saying that! (*Pause, mocks him.*) "I'm dying! I'm dying!" Good God—what a maudlin son-of-a-bitch you've turned out to be. What's happened to you? Have you been laying around here, feeling sorry for yourself? Moping in the dark? In *my* bed!

*Pause.*

CARTER: I can't get my pants on.

VINNIE: Jesus Christ!

CARTER: I can't.

VINNIE: Here—let me help you.

VINNIE *goes to him and holds his pants while* CARTER *attempts to put his legs in.*

VINNIE: Stop shaking and lift your leg! Just stop all that shaking and chattering.

CARTER (*as he tries to lift his leg*): I'm not going back there, you know.

VINNIE: Just lift your leg up!

CARTER: I'm not.

VINNIE: All right, you're not going back there. That's fine. You need to get dressed first.

CARTER: I'm not going back, Vinnie.

VINNIE: Will you lift your goddamn leg!

CARTER: I'm staying here.

VINNIE *grabs his leg and forces it into the pants as* CARTER *hangs onto his shoulder. They struggle for balance, with the pants, going in small circles.*

CARTER: I'm going to change my name.

VINNIE: Good.

CARTER: I'm going to disappear.

VINNIE: That's great.

CARTER: I'm going to stay here with you.

VINNIE: No, you're not.

CARTER: I'll pay half the rent.

VINNIE: You're paying *all* of it now.

CARTER: I'll pay half.

VINNIE: Pull your pants up! Pull them up!

VINNIE *turns loose of him and lets* CARTER *crash to the floor with his pants half way up. Pause.* VINNIE *watches him as* CARTER *crawls towards the blanket and reaches for it.*

VINNIE: You're not staying here, Carter. You're not staying here with me, if that's what you think. Where'd you ever get an idea like that?

CARTER (*pulling blanket around him*): We could maybe start up with the claimers again. Start brand new.

VINNIE: Those days are over, Carter. Long gone. Give it up.

CARTER: We made a couple a' mistakes. A couple a' bad mistakes.

VINNIE: Mistakes?

CARTER: Yeah. I admit that.

VINNIE: That's big of you.

CARTER: But we had a—partnership going there for a while. A real parternship. We were like—a team. We had a feeling between us. Didn't we, Vinnie? A real feeling.

*Pause.* VINNIE *moves toward bed, unbuttoning his shirt.*

VINNIE: I'm gonna lay down, Carter. I'm gonna lay down and I'm gonna fall asleep. I'm not gonna dream, I'm just gonna sleep. And when I wake up, I want you gone.

CARTER: I'll make you a deal then.

VINNIE: Sure. A deal. Another deal.

CARTER: I'll swap you straight across the board.

VINNIE: Swap me? Swap me for what?

CARTER: I'll take your place and you can have mine.

VINNIE: You're delirious. Why are you acting like this? It's time for you to go home, Carter!

VINNIE *sits on bed and starts taking off his shoes.*

CARTER: You can have it all. Even Rosie.

VINNIE: I don't want it all. I don't want anything you've got. You can stop sending me all your bullshit. All your TVs and Jap cars and corny golf shirts. All your guilt money. You can keep all that. Now if you don't get up off my floor, I'm gonna drag your ass out into the road and leave you there. I'm just gonna leave you laying out there, rolling and shaking and frothing at the mouth.

You can die with your tongue hanging out. I don't give a shit. Just get up off my floor! NOW!!

VINNIE *leaps at him from the bed and rips the blanket off* CARTER. *Pause as* VINNIE *hovers menacingly over him then returns to bed. He pulls the cardboard boxes out from under bed and starts taking out all his detective gear and putting it on: his shoulder holster and pistol, his badge, handcuffs, sneakers and overcoat.* CARTER *watches him from the floor.*

CARTER: What're you doing?

VINNIE: I'm going out to get a bottle.

CARTER: Now? You're not going to just leave me here, are you?

VINNIE: Yeah. That's what I'm gonna do.

CARTER: Wait a minute, Vinnie—

VINNIE: If you're not gone when I get back, I'm going to put you on the highway. In your underwear.

CARTER: Wait a second. Wait a second, Vinnie. This thing's bound to pass. I just need a little recovery time.

VINNIE: Time's up, partner.

CARTER: Let me stay here with you, Vinnie.

VINNIE: There's only one bed. And that's mine.

CARTER: I'll get a cot. A mattress, or something.

VINNIE: There's no room.

CARTER: I'll stay out of your way. I promise. I'll keep to myself. I'll stay completely—separate. If—If you have a girlfriend come over or something—If that Cecilia girl comes over, I'll—I'll go out on the lawn. I'll sleep out there. On the front lawn. I promise, Vinnie. I'll disappear. It'll be like—you won't even know I'm around.

VINNIE *has all his detective gear on by now. He moves to* CARTER *and stops, standing over him. Pause.*

VINNIE: I'll know.

CARTER: You're not gonna go out now, are you? I thought you were tired.

VINNIE: I'm suddenly inspired.

CARTER: What're you gonna do out there?

VINNIE: Surveillance. I'm working on a new case. It's a great feeling to embark on a case. It fills me with purpose. I'm my own man again. I move wherever I want to. I answer to no one. I cut through backyards and they never even know I'm there. I see it all, Carter. I'm a witness to it all. I see it through their windows. I see how helpless they all are. How they're all in the grips of something. And the great thing about this business is there's no end to it. It's bottomless. Just imagine that. Right now, right this very second, someone is cutting someone else's throat. It's amazing.

CARTER: Let me stay here just for a little while, Vinnie.

VINNIE: Go back home, Carter. The kids are waiting. It's Halloween.

VINNIE *exits, leaving* CARTER *alone on the floor. Pause as* CARTER *looks around the space. His chills intensify. He scrambles toward the blanket and wraps it around his shoulders. He holds himself across the chest and rocks slowly back and forth.*

CECILIA *enters from stage right with her purse still stuffed with* CARTER'S *money and* VINNIE'S *laundry all clean and folded. She's still wearing her Derby dress. She stops and stares at* CARTER. *He turns quickly toward her, shaking. Pause.*

CECILIA *crosses to the bed and sets* VINNIE'*s clean laundry on it. She turns towards* CARTER *with purse. She goes to* CARTER *and begins to take fistfuls of money out of purse and drops the money in front of* CARTER *in a pile.*

CECILIA: Your money's all here. You can count it if you want to. I only used a little bit for sandwiches and tea. I'll pay you back, I promise. You should have told me the Derby was in May, Mr Carter. Why would you lie about something as simple as that?

CARTER'*s phone begins to ring. They both stare at it.*

CECILIA: Do you want me to answer that?

*Pause.* CARTER *just stares at phone.* CECILIA *moves to exit, stops and turns back to* CARTER. *Pause.*

CECILIA: Somebody ought to answer that.

*She exits. Phone keeps ringing.* CARTER *keeps staring at it without moving to answer. He shakes in his blanket as lights dim slowly. Phone rings into the blackness then stops.*